THE

WRINKLIES' WIT & WISDOM

Thousands of humorous quotes about getting on a bit

COMPILED BY

Rosemarie Jarski, Allison Vale

& Alison Rattle

Published in Great Britain in 2008 by
PRION
an imprint of the
Carlton Publishing Group
20 Mortimer Street
London W1T 3JW

3 5 7 9 10 8 6 4

The material in this book was previously published in *Wrinklies' Wit and Wisdom* and *Wrinklies' Wit and Wisdom Forever*

A catalogue record for this book is available from the British Library

ISBN 978-1-85375-670-2

Typeset by E-Type, Liverpool
Printed in the UK by CPI Mackays, Chatham, ME5 8TD

Contents

With mirth and laughter let old wrinkles come.

William Shakespeare

Introduction

Last year a company which looks into social trends carried out a survey called 'Understanding Fiftysomethings'. Seventeen hundred people, ranging in age from 45 to 89, were questioned about all aspects of their lives. Part of the research invited participants to send in a photograph: 'a snapshot of your life'. On the cover of the final report was a picture of a wheelchair and a Zimmer frame with these words: 'Among 600 snaps taken by older Britons, we found just one like this. So why is it one of the first images to spring to mind when someone mentions old age?' Pictures submitted included a pair of cowboy boots, a computer, a brochure for hip hotels, a pair of Gina high heels, a bottle of wine, and several packets of Rowntree's jelly.

What this reveals – beyond the pleasing fact that a love of jelly lingers on into one's dotage – is the sheer diversity of older people today. Traditional stereotypes of knitting grannies and doddering grandpas just aren't true anymore (if, indeed, they ever were). Older people dress up, drink wine, travel, surf the net, send texts, have sex. The baby-boomer generation has redefined the meaning of 'old'. Grey is the new black! Saga-louts are the new lager-louts! Old is the new young!

Or is it?

Introduction

Old myths die hard. Senior citizens may have changed but the rest of society has yet to notice. The clichéd image of old age is still common currency in our culture. Media and advertising (run by tots barely free of nappy-rash) still lump all older people into one homogenous group. This group is then routinely mocked, trivialized, patronized, or ignored altogether. The over-60s represent over 20 per cent of the population but they feature in only nine per cent of advertisements and television coverage. The charity Age Concern ran a billboard poster showing the head of a grey-haired man with the caption: 'Ignore this poster. It's got grey hair'. Newspapers and magazines are littered with insidious remarks that undermine or belittle older people. Casual comments like, 'she's on the wrong side of 50', 'he may be in his 60s but…', 'he's still going strong, despite being 56' may seem innocuous, but multiply them by hundreds of similar comments day after day and they add up to one thing: ageism.

Ageism is entrenched in our society. In the National Health Service, younger patients are up to twice as likely as older ones to receive the best available treatment. Older patients are also more likely to get a DNR - 'Do Not Resuscitate'. The charity Age Concern highlighted the case of an elderly lady who died in hospital and was found to have NFR ('Not For Resuscitation') written across her toes. If this was racism or sexism there would be riots on the streets and questions in Parliament, but because it's 'only old folk' such scandalous treatment elicits barely more than a raised eyebrow.

The test of a civilized society is how it treats its older citizens. 'It is easy to love children,' writes Abraham Heschel, 'even tyrants and dictators make a point of being fond of children. But the affection and care for the old, the incurable, the helpless are the true gold mines of a culture.' In the United Kingdom, twice as many people give to charities that help animals as those who give to charities supporting older people.

To find respect and deference towards age you have to look beyond Western culture to Asian and African nations. Margaret Simey, a suffragette in the 1920s and local councillor for more than 20 years, was shocked and dismayed to discover that after her retirement she was slung out onto the scrap heap by society and became a non-person. Then she paid a visit to her son in the southern African kingdom of Lesotho: 'I found myself greeted with enthusiasm by the villagers. Pleased but baffled by my reception, I was told on inquiry that what moved them was their pleasure that my son should enjoy the exceptional good fortune of having such an old mother. To them, my experience and wisdom were worth more than money in the bank.' The Third World has much to teach us about the Third Age.

Similarly, in Japan, reverence for old age is ingrained in their culture and their psyche. As Barbara Bloom observes: 'When the Japanese mend broken objects they aggrandize the damage by filling the cracks with gold, because they believe that when something's suffered damage and has a history it becomes more beautiful.'

Any society that doesn't value its older citizens is off its rocker. We're all getting older, so ageism is like turkeys voting for Christmas. Ignorance and fear are at the root of it. Dread of our own deterioration and mortality leads to fear and revulsion of old people who are reminders of that inevitability.

Making role models of celebrities doesn't help. None fear the ageing process more than they. Celebrities may pay collagen-enhanced-lip-service to growing old gracefully, but then they sneak off to the plastic surgeon's to be nipped, tucked and liposuctioned to within an inch of their livers. They line up to go on *Oprah* to share their drink, drug and sex addictions but how many will 'fess up to a face-lift? There's a saying in Hollywood: 'The second worst sin is to be old; the worst is to look old.' The mother of Zsa Zsa Gabor was still having cosmetic surgery in her 90s. Before going under the knife she instructed her surgeon to complete the procedure even if she died on the operating table.

Let's face it, when it comes to ageing, our society needs to fundamentally rethink its attitudes – and fast. Advances in preventative medicine and improved nutrition mean we're staying healthy and living longer. By 2030, one-third of the entire population of the UK will be over 60. Centenarians are the world's fastest-growing age group, and scientists predict that millennium babies can expect to live to be 130.

Great news. But what's the point of these extra years if all we can look forward to are discrimination, derision and yet more adverts for life insurance ('No medical, and no salesman will call')? Life is not just about staying alive but *living*. What we need are better role models, less hypocrisy, more honesty, an end to the obsession with youth, an education programme to teach the younger generation to value experience and wisdom, and a more accurate reflection of what life is like after the free bus pass.

A collection of wrinklies' wit and wisdom can't change the world; the best it can do is to fly the flag for wrinklies everywhere. Gilded youth is swept aside as golden oldies take centre-stage. But that's not to say that the young can't also find enjoyment – and enlightenment – here. This is a book for anyone who's getting older. John Mortimer, *The Golden Girls*, Barry Cryer, Bill Crosby and Elaine Stritch are inspirational role models for any age. They never pass their amuse-by dates; their wisdom is timeless. Most of the contributors can ride the buses for free so they speak with the voice of experience. They shoot from the hip – real or titanium – sharing the pleasures as well as what Byron called 'the woes that wait on age'.

Wrapping those woes in wit doesn't make them go away, but it does make them a bit more bearable. If laughter is the best medicine, consider this the perfect prescription for ageing well and living a full and happy life. Pop a few pearls of wit and wisdom every day and that telegram from Her Majesty is practically in the bag. You see, he who laughs, lasts.

Age Is Just a Number

I'm very pleased to be here. Let's face it, at my age I'm pleased to be anywhere.

George Burns X

He was either a man of about 150 who was rather young for his years, or a man of about 110 who had been aged by trouble.

P. G. Wodehouse

I'm as old as my tongue and a little bit older than my teeth.

Kris Kringle, Miracle on 34th Street

Age is a question of mind over matter. If you don't mind, age don't matter.

Satchel Paige

We're obsessed with age. Numbers are always and pointlessly attached to every name that's published in a newspaper: 'Joe Creamer, 43, and his daughter,

Tiffany-Ann, 9, were merrily chasing a bunny, 2, when Tiffany-Ann tripped on the root of a tree, 106.'

Joan Rivers

People who define themselves by their age are about as appealing to be with as feminists who drone on about women's rights, homosexuals who are obsessed with being gay, or environmentalists who mention recycling every time they drop by for green tea.

Marcelle D'Argy-Smith

Exactly how old is Joan Collins? We need an expert. Someone who counts the rings on trees.

Ruby Wax

Let's just say I reached the age of consent 75,000 consents ago.

Shelley Winters

My sister, Jackie, is younger than me. We don't know quite by how much.

Joan Collins

I don't know how old I am because the goat ate the Bible that had my birth certificate in it. The goat lived to be 27.

Satchel Paige

Age is something that doesn't matter, unless you are a cheese.

Billie Burke

Age only matters when one is ageing. Now that I have arrived at a great age, I might just as well be 20.

Pablo Picasso

I'm 80, but in my own mind, my age veers. When I'm performing on stage, I'm 40; when I'm shopping in Waitrose, I'm 120.

Humphrey Lyttelton

I'm 42 around the chest, 52 around the waist, 92 around the golf course and a nuisance around the house.

Groucho Marx

When I turned 2 I was really anxious, because I'd doubled my age in a year. I thought, if this keeps up, by the time I'm six I'll be 90.

Steven Wright

How old would you be if you didn't know how old you were?

Satchel Paige

Age Is Just a Number

I have no romantic feelings about age. Either you are interesting at any age or you are not. There is nothing particularly interesting about being old – or being young, for that matter.

Katharine Hepburn

'When I was your age...' No one is ever anyone else's age, except physically.

Faith Baldwin

It is a sobering thought that when Mozart was my age he had been dead for two years.

Tom Lehrer

I am just turning 40 and taking my time about it.

Harold Lloyd, 77

I can't believe I'm 30. Do you know how much that is in gay years?

Jack McFarland, Will and Grace

I am past 30, and three parts iced over.

Matthew Arnold

If you want to know how old a woman is, ask her sister-in-law.

Ed Howe

I refuse to admit that I'm more than 52, even if that does make my sons illegitimate.

Nancy Astor

The years that a woman subtracts from her age are not lost. They are added to the ages of other women.

Diane de Poitiers

I can lie convincingly about my age because at my age I can't always remember what it is.

Violet Conti

When I hit 55 I decided to start telling people I was older so they would compliment me on how young I looked for my age. But I was hoist by my own petard when the first person I told I was 60 laid a sympathetic hand on my shoulder and said, 'Not to worry, we old timers must stick together!'

Lydia Martinez

Thirty is a nice age for a woman. Especially if she happens to be 40.

Phyllis Diller

A woman telling her true age is like a buyer confiding his final price to an Armenian rug dealer.

Mignon McLaughlin

Age Is Just a Number

I have always felt that a woman has the right to treat the subject of her age with ambiguity until, perhaps, she passes into the realm beyond 90. Then it is better that she be candid with herself and with the world.

Helena Rubinstein

Never trust a woman who tells one her real age. A woman who would tell one that, would tell anything.

Oscar Wilde

A woman is as old as she looks before breakfast.

Ed Howe

She may very well pass for 43 in the dusk with the light behind her!

W. S. Gilbert

If the Nobel Prize were awarded by a woman, it would go to the inventor of the dimmer switch.

Kathy Lette

– Age is nothing but a state of mind.
– Tell that to my thighs.

Dorothy Zbornak and Blanche Devereaux, The Golden Girls

A woman is as young as her knees.

Mary Quant

People who say you're just as old as you feel are all wrong, fortunately.

Russell Baker

The best thing to do is to behave in a manner befitting one's age. If you are 16 or under, try not to go bald.

Woody Allen

The worst thing anyone has ever said about me is that I'm 50. Which I am. Oh that bitch. I was so hurt.

Joan Rivers

The real sadness of being 50 is not that you change so much but that you change so little.

Max Lerner

Whenever the talk turns to age, I say I am 49 plus VAT.

Lionel Blair

The years between 50 and 70 are the hardest. You are always being asked to do things, and you are not yet decrepit enough to turn them down.

T. S. Eliot

I'm 52 years of age now but I prefer to think of myself as 11 centigrade.

Tom Lehrer

Age Is Just a Number

The war years count double. Things and people not actively in use age twice as fast.

Arnold Bennett

I recently turned 60. Practically a third of my life is over.

Woody Allen

I have been a success: for 60 years I have eaten, and have avoided being eaten.

Logan Pearsall Smith

Here I sit, alone and 60, bald and fat and full of sin; cold the seat and loud the cistern, as I read the Harpic tin.

Alan Bennett

At the end of this year, I shall be 63 – if alive – and about the same if dead.

Mark Twain

Will you still need me, will you still feed me, when I'm 64?

Paul McCartney & John Lennon

I'll never make the mistake of turning 70 again.

Casey Stengel

It is better to be 70 years young than 40 years old.

Oliver Wendell Holmes

If it's true that 50 is the new 30, then it follows that 70 is the new 50.

Joan Collins

You don't realize what fine fighting material there is in age. You show me anyone who's lived to over 70 and you show me a fighter – someone who's got the will to live.

Agatha Christie

I'm 78. The late Ronnie Scott used to ask people their age and would respond, in his hard-edged way: 'Really! You don't look a day over (in my case) 79!' A good corrective, which I resort to when I feel sorry for myself.

George Melly

Eighty's a landmark and people treat you differently than they do when you're 79. At 79, if you drop something it just lies there. At 80, people pick it up for you.

Helen Van Slyke

Age Is Just a Number

In a dream you are never 80.

Anne Sexton

There must be a day or two in a man's life when he is the precise age for something important.

Franklin Pierce Adams

The life expectancy now is 72 for men, and 75 or 76 or something for women. It's amazing to think that just a couple thousand years ago, life expectancy was 30, which in our terms would be that you get your driver's licence around 5, get married at 9, divorced at 15, in your late teens you move down to Florida.

Jerry Seinfeld

If a Renaissance or Georgian man could return he would be as much astonished by the sight of two or three thousand septuagenarians and octogenarians lining a south-coast resort on a summer's day, as he would by a television set. His was a world where it was the exception to be grey.

Ronald Blythe

It is so comic to hear oneself called old, even at 90, I suppose!

Alice James

Age puzzles me. I thought it was a quiet time. My 70s were interesting and fairly serene, but my 80s are passionate. I grow more intense as I age.

Florida Scott-Maxwell

The hardest years in life are those between 10 and 70.

Helen Hayes

There's one advantage to being 102. No peer pressure.

Dennis Wolfberg

People under 24 think old age starts around 55, those over 75, on the other hand, believe that youth doesn't end until the age of 58.

Alexander Chancellor

I'm 65 and I guess that puts me in with the geriatrics. But if there were 15 months in every year, I'd only be 48. That's the trouble with us. We number everything. Take women, for example. I think they deserve to have more than 12 years between the ages of 28 and 40.

James Thurber

No one is so old as to think he cannot live one more year.

Marcus T. Cicero

Age Is Just a Number

No woman should ever be quite accurate about her age. It looks so calculating.

Oscar Wilde

Who wants to be 95? 94-year-olds.

George Burns

The age of a woman doesn't mean a thing. The best tunes are played on the oldest fiddles.

Ralph Waldo Emerson

Autumn is really the best of seasons; and I'm not sure that old age isn't the best part of life.

C. S. Lewis

I'm not interested in age. People who tell me their age are silly. You're as old as you feel.

Elizabeth Arden

Like many women my age, I am 28 years old.

Mary Schmitt

The seven ages of man: spills, drills, thrills, bills, ills, pills and wills.

Richard John Needham

How the hell should I know? Most of the people my age are dead.

Casey Stengel, on the subject of his age

Age ain't nothin' but a number. But age is other things, too. It is wisdom, if one has lived one's life properly. It is experience and knowledge. And it is getting to know all the ways the world turns, so that if you cannot turn the world the way you want, you can at least get out of the way so you won't get run over.

Miriam Makeba

A sexagenarian? At his age? I think that's disgusting.

Gracie Allen

You can judge your age by the amount of pain you feel when you come in contact with a new idea.

John Nuveen

I do wish I could tell you my age but it's impossible. It keeps changing all the time.

Greer Garson

I am luminous with age.

Meridel Le Sueur

Age Is Just a Number

Age is not measured by years. Nature does not equally distribute energy. Some people are born old and tired while others are going strong at 70.

Dorothy Thompson

Your 50s are mature, reliable and dependable – or boring, predictable and conventional.

T. Kinnes

Old age is a special problem for me because I've never been able to shed the mental image I have of myself – a lad of about 19.

E. B. White

I'm 57. I can't look like a 30-year-old. You try to hold age at bay, but there comes a point when you just have to give up gracefully.

Elton John

The biggest disadvantage of old age is that you can't outgrow it.

Anon

Old age brings along with its uglinesses the comfort that you will soon be out of it – which ought to be a substantial relief to such discontented pendulums as we are.

Ralph Waldo Emerson

You can calculate Zsa Zsa Gabor's age by the rings on her fingers.

Bob Hope

At 65 and drawing a state pension, I was delighted to discover that only people under 45 would regard me as old, even though sadly nobody would actually call me young.

Alexander Chancellor

Nobody knows the age of the human race, but everybody agrees that it is old enough to know better.

Anon

Age is whatever you think it is. You are as old as you think you are.

Muhammad Ali

When you get to my age you either run away or jump in with both feet.

Jan Leeming

I think all this talk about age is foolish. Every time I'm one year older, everyone else is too.

Gloria Swanson

Age is not a handicap. Age is nothing but a number. It is how you use it.

Diesel Payne

Nobody grows old by merely living a number of years. People grow old only by deserting their ideals. Years wrinkle the face, but to give up enthusiasm wrinkles the soul.

Anon

Age is just a number. It's totally irrelevant unless, of course, you happen to be a bottle of wine.

Joan Collins

Growing Old Is...

...when 'getting lucky' means finding your car in the car park.

...when an 'all-nighter' means not getting up to pee.

...when 'getting a little action' means you don't need to eat any fibre.

...when you're told to slow down by the doctor instead of the police.

...when going bra-less pulls all the wrinkles out of your face.

...when a sexy babe catches your attention and your pacemaker opens the garage door.

...when your friends compliment you on your new alligator shoes and you're barefoot.

...when you remember when it cost more to run a car than to park it.

All Anon

...when you've met so many people that every new person you meet reminds you of someone else.

Ogden Nash

Youthful Thinking

I never felt that there was anything enviable in youth. I cannot recall that any of us, as youths, admired our condition to excess or had a desire to prolong it.

Bernard Berenson

Youthful Thinking

Zeal, n. A certain nervous disorder afflicting the young and inexperienced.

Ambrose Bierce

Youth would be an ideal state if it came a little later in life.

Herbert Asquith

Youth is a wonderful thing. What a crime to waste it on children.

George Bernard Shaw

American youth attributes much more importance to arriving at driver's licence age than at voting age.

Marshall McLuhan

When we are young we are slavishly employed in procuring something whereby we may live comfortably when we grow old; and when we are old, we perceive it is too late to live as we proposed.

Alexander Pope

It is better to waste one's youth than to do nothing with it at all.

Georges Courteline

I'm aiming by the time I'm 50 to stop being an adolescent.

Wendy Cope

I live in that solitude which is painful in youth, but delicious in the years of maturity.

Albert Einstein

Youth is like spring, an overpraised season.

Samuel Butler

Old age at least gives me an excuse for not being very good at things that I was not very good at when I was young.

Thomas Sowell

We are only young once. That is all society can stand.

Bob Bowen

When you are young, you want to be the master of your fate and the captain of your soul. When you are older, you will settle for being the master of your weight and the captain of your bowling team.

Anon

In youth we run into difficulties. In old age difficulties run into us.

Beverly Sills

You're only as old as you feel… but you can't be Shirley Temple on the *Good Ship Lollipop* forever. Sooner or later, dammit, you're old.

Joan Crawford

If youth knew; if age could.

Henri Estienne

The Seven Ages of Man

The seven ages of man have become preschooler, Pepsi generation, baby boomer, mid-lifer, empty-nester, senior citizen, and organ donor.

Bill Cosby

The three ages of man: youth, middle age, and 'You're looking wonderful!'

Dore Schary

There are three stages of man: he believes in Santa Claus; he does not believe in Santa Claus; he is Santa Claus.

Bob Phillips

There are only three ages for women in Hollywood: *Babe, District Attorney*, and *Driving Miss Daisy*.

Goldie Hawn

Your 40s, you grow a little potbelly, you grow another chin. The music starts to get too loud and one of your old girlfriends from high school becomes a grandmother. Your 50s, you have a minor surgery. You'll call it a procedure, but it's a surgery. Your 60s, you have a major surgery, the music is still loud but it doesn't matter because you can't hear it anyway. 70s, you and the wife retire to Fort Lauderdale, you start eating dinner at two, lunch around 10, breakfast the night before. And you spend most of your time wandering around malls looking for the ultimate in soft yoghurt and muttering 'How come the kids don't call?' By your 80s, you've had a major stroke, and you end up babbling to some Jamaican nurse who your wife can't stand but who you call mama. Any questions?

Mitch Robbins, City Slickers

My mother used to say the seven ages were: childhood, adolescence, adulthood, middle age, elderly, old, and wonderful.

Mary Wilson

I think the life cycle is all backwards. You should die first, get it out of the way. Then you live in an old age home. You get kicked out when you're too young, you get a gold watch, you go to work. You work 40 years until you're young enough to enjoy your retirement.

You do drugs, alcohol, you party, you get ready for high school. You go to grade school, you become a kid, you play, you have no responsibilities, you become a little baby, you go back into the womb, you spend your last nine months floating … and you finish off as an orgasm.

George Carlin

Be on the alert to recognize your prime at whatever time of your life it may occur.

Miss Jean Brodie, The Prime of Miss Jean Brodie, *Muriel Spark*

It has begun to occur to me that life is a stage I'm going through.

Ellen Goodman

Old Women...

...will never wake you in the middle of the night to ask, 'What are you thinking?' They don't care what you think.

...look good in bright-red lipstick, unlike younger women and drag queens.

...have lived long enough to know how to please a

man in ways their daughters could never dream of.
...develop a well-honed sixth sense as they age. They instinctively know when you've goofed up.

...are genetically superior: for every spectacular babe of 70 there is a rotund and receding relic in yellow plaid pants flirting ridiculously with the 22-year-old waitress.

All Anon

...are best, because they always think they may be doing it for the last time.

Ian Fleming

Whenever I see an old lady slip and fall on a wet sidewalk, my first instinct is to laugh. But then I think, what if I was an ant, and she fell on me. Then it wouldn't seem quite so funny.

Jack Handey

...are like ageing strudels – the crust may not be so lovely, but the filling has come at last into its own.

Robert Farrar Capon

Some turn to vinegar, but the best improve with age.

C. E. M. Joad

Time and trouble will tame an advanced woman, but an advanced old woman is uncontrollable by any earthly force.

Dorothy L. Sayers

What's more beautiful than an old lady with white hair, grown wise with age and able to tell lovely stories about her past?

Brigitte Bardot

There are three classes into which all the women past 70 that ever I knew were to be divided: 1. That dear old soul; 2. That old woman; 3. That old witch.

Samuel Taylor Coleridge

If you want a thing done well, get a couple of old broads to do it.

Bette Davis

Old Men...

...have so much more to offer than young guys. They've done all their running and sown all their wild oats.

Celine Dion

...fall asleep in the middle of television programmes for no apparent reason. In the middle of conversations, actually, or is that just me? One minute there's an adult person you're engaging with on some vaguely cerebral level, and the next minute there's somebody quietly snoring.

Kathryn Flett, Grumpy Old Women

...can be short and dumpy and getting bald but if [they have] fire, women will like [them].

Mae West

...are only walking hospitals.

Wentworth Dillon

Old People

Old people don't need companionship. They need to be isolated and studied so it can be determined what nutrients they have that might be extracted for our personal use.

Homer Simpson

At the Harvest Festival in church the area behind the pulpit was piled high with tins of IXL fruit for the old-age pensioners. We had collected the tinned fruit from door to door. Most of it came from old-age pensioners.

Clive James

Old people do more scandalous things than any rebel you want to name. Because they don't give a damn. They couldn't give a rat's ass what you think. They're 80 years old. They're leaving soon, you know what I mean?

Chris Isaak

It would be a good thing if young people were wise, and old people were strong, but God has arranged things better.

Martin Luther

The great secret that all old people share is that you really haven't changed in 70 or 80 years. Your body changes, but you don't change at all. And that, of course, causes great confusion.

Doris Lessing

Happy Birthday to You?

Two weeks ago we celebrated my uncle's 103rd birthday. 103 – isn't that something? Unfortunately he wasn't present. How could he be? He died when he was 29.

Victor Borge

Like a hole in the head I need another birthday.

Dorothy Parker

For all the advances in medicine, there is still no cure for the common birthday.

John Glenn

A diplomat is a man who always remembers a woman's birthday but never remembers her age.

Robert Frost

Birthdays are nature's way of telling us to eat more cake.

Jo Brand

Birthdays are good for you. Statistics show that the people who have the most live the longest.

Larry Lorenzoni

I had a huge party for my 70th birthday with 800 guests. With so many familiar faces there, it was like driving through the rear-view mirror.

Peter Ustinov

Buying presents for old people is a problem. I would rather like it if people came to my house and took things away.

Clement Freud

Happy Birthday to You?

I was invited to Hugh Hefner's 75th birthday party but I couldn't figure out what gift to buy him. What do you give the man who's had everyone? Then I thought of it: monogrammed Viagra!

David Letterman

What would I like for my 87th birthday? A paternity suit.

George Burns

—Be honest, Victor, I bet this was the last birthday present you were expecting.
—Yes, it was. It's ermmm … a gravestone.
—Yes. You haven't already got one? Obviously I haven't filled in the date of death yet, but if and when – Margaret can just give me a shout.

George and Victor Meldrew, One Foot in the Grave

Last week the candle factory burned down. Everyone just stood around and sang Happy Birthday.

Steven Wright

Most of us can remember a time when a birthday, especially if it was one's own, brightened the world as if a second sun had risen.

Robert Lynd

It is lovely, when I forget all birthdays, including my own, to find that somebody remembers me.

Ellen Glasgow

The formula for youth: Keep your enthusiasm and forget your birthdays.

Anon

Don't send funny greeting cards on birthdays or at Christmas. Save them for funerals when their cheery effect is needed.

P.J. O'Rourke

What ought to be done to the man who invented the celebrating of anniversaries? Mere killing would be too light.

Mark Twain

I always add a year to myself, so I'm prepared for my next birthday. So when I was 39, I was already 40.

Nicolas Cage

When I was a kid I could toast marshmallows over my birthday candles. Now I could roast a turkey!

Anon

There comes a time when you should stop expecting other people to make a big deal about your birthday. That time is age 11.

Dave Barry

Is that a birthday? 'Tis, alas! too clear; 'tis but the funeral of the former year.

Alexander Pope

When a man has a birthday, he takes a day off. When a woman has a birthday, she takes at least three years off.

Joan Rivers

The best birthdays of all are those that haven't arrived yet.

Robert Orben

From our birthday, until we die, is but the winking of an eye.

William Butler Yeats

Last year my birthday cake looked like a prairie fire.

Rodney Dangerfield

Growing Old

—You know what the worst part about getting old is?
—Your face?

Blanche Devereaux and Dorothy Zbornak, The Golden Girls

Growing old is like being increasingly penalized for a crime you haven't committed.

Anthony Powell

Age to women is like kryptonite to Superman.

Kathy Lette

There is absolutely nothing to be said in favour of growing old. There ought to be legislation against it.

Patrick Moore

In the middle of the 19th century, an Englishman named Robert Browning wrote: 'Grow old along with me, the best is yet to be.' Clearly this man was a minor poet. Or else he wrote those lines when he was 12.

Joan Rivers

I am not 'of a certain age', Niles. I am smack dab in the middle of 'not a kid anymore'. I won't be 'of a certain age' for another 10 years.

Frasier Crane, Frasier

Frasier, you may think it's tough being middle-aged but think about me – I've got a son who's middle-aged.

Martin Crane, Frasier

Growing Old

Middle age is when you're sitting at home on Saturday night and the telephone rings and you hope it isn't for you.

Ogden Nash

I am at that age. Too young for the bowling green, too old for Ecstasy.

Rab C. Nesbitt

One problem with growing older is that it gets increasingly tougher to find a famous historical figure who didn't amount to much when he was your age.

Bill Vaughan

There are days of oldness, and then one gets young again. It goes backward and forward, not in one direction.

Katharine Hathaway

People want you to be like you were in 1969. They want you to be, because otherwise their youth goes with you.

Mick Jagger

Only two things improve with age: wine and Susan Sarandon.

Boyd Farrow

Jameson's Irish Whiskey really does improve with age: the older I get the more I like it.

Bob Monkhouse

When I was elected to the European Parliament, I was invited to join its Committee on Ageing. The very words put years on me and I refused, saying that the only committee in which I might be interested would be a committee on keeping young.

Barbara Castle

I don't believe that one grows older. I think that what happens early on in life is that at a certain age one stands still and stagnates.

T. S. Eliot

There are people whose watch stops at a certain hour and who remain permanently at that age.

Charles Augustin Sainte-Beuve

Many people die at 25 and aren't buried until they are 75.

Max Frisch

Colleagues of Margaret Thatcher have rejected criticism that she is now a pale reflection of her former self because, as they recall it, she never had a reflection.

Dead Ringers

Growing Old

Growing old is no more than a bad habit which a busy man has not time to form.

André Maurois

When friends pressed her to carry a walking stick, Princess Alice reluctantly agreed, but she had it disguised as an umbrella.

R.W. Apple

She had finally reached the age where she was more afraid of getting old than dying.

Julia Phillips

Why do we get older? Why do our bodies wear out? Why can't we just go on and on, accumulating a potentially infinite number of Frequent Flier mileage points?

Dave Barry

I'm 43, and for the first time this year I have felt older. I'm slowly becoming more decrepit. I think you just move to the country and wear an old fleece.

Jennifer Saunders

Old age and sickness bring out the essential characteristics of a man.

Felix Frankfurter

It's sad to grow old, but nice to ripen.

Brigitte Bardot

The best way to adjust – no, ignore – most of the negative thoughts about ageing is to say to yourself, with conviction, 'I am still the very same person I have been all of my adult life.' You are, you know.

Helen Hayes

A good old age can be the crown of our life's experience, the masterwork of a lifetime.

Helen Nearing

Oh, I was so much older then; I'm younger than that now.

Bob Dylan

Growing old is something you do if you're lucky.

Groucho Marx

When the Pope Starts Looking Young

SIGNS YOU'RE GETTING OLD

There are three signs of old age: loss of memory … I forget the other two.

Red Skelton

When the Pope Starts Looking Young

You will recognize, my boy, the first sign of old age: it is when you go out into the streets of London and realize for the first time how young the policemen look.

Seymour Hicks

Do you think policemen walk up and down the street thinking how old the public are getting these days?

D. Tucker

You know you're getting old when high court judges start looking young to you.

Ronnie Golden

I knew I was getting old when the Pope started looking young.

Billy Wilder

An uncle of mine, a retired headmaster, said that the first time he felt old was when he was in a queue at his local post office to collect his old age pension and found himself behind a former pupil who was there for the same purpose.

Paul Kelvin-Smith

True terror is to wake up one morning and discover that your high-school class is running the country.

Kurt Vonnegut

When the Pope Starts Looking Young

Whenever a man's friends begin to compliment him about looking young, he may be sure that they think he is growing old.

Washington Irving

I was in a coffee shop doing a survey for free drinks. The age bracket tick-boxes were: 16–21; 21–27; 27–35; 35–50. I am over 50 and I realized I am one tick-box away from death.

Anon

A British Gas salesman, replacing a defective boiler, told me: 'The makers will tell you this boiler will give 25 years' service.' He looked up at me, hesitated, and continued, 'But of course to you that would not be a selling point.'

Kenneth Bruce, 78

I've started wearing cardigans and saying things like 'Whoopsadaisy', and when I take a first sip of tea, 'Ooh, that hits the spot!'

Gary, Men Behaving Badly

If, at the age of 30, you are stiff and out of shape, then you are old. If, at 60, you are supple and strong, then you are young.

Joseph Pilates

When the Pope Starts Looking Young

Signs you're getting on a bit: your back hurts; you eat food past its sell-by date; your carpet is patterned; you go supermarket shopping in the evening to pick up marked-down bargains; you can spell; you hang your clothes on padded coat hangers; you save the hearing aid flyer that falls out of the colour supplement; you try to get electrical gadgets repaired when they go wrong; you save the free little packets of sugar from cafés; you have worn a knitted swimsuit; when you watch black-and-white films you spend the whole time pointing at the screen going, 'He's dead ... She's dead ...'; your car stereo is tuned to Radio 2.

Colin Slater

You know you're getting older if you have more fingers than real teeth.

Rodney Dangerfield

One of the signs of old age is that you have to carry your senses around in your handbag – glasses, hearing aid, dentures, etc.

Kurt Strauss

I contemplated buying a new cream that claimed to stop the seven signs of ageing and wondered what they might be. Incontinence? Talking about the weather? Wearing slippers? Memory loss? Compulsive need to queue up at the post office? Memory loss? Inability to comprehend the lyrics of pop songs?

Maria McErlane

I first felt old walking in Spain with my 13-year-old daughter when I belatedly realized the wolf-whistle was not for me.

Adele Thorpe

I know I must be getting old because I saw a young lady with her midriff showing and thought, 'Ooh, you must be cold.'

John Marsh

You know you're getting old when you feel like the day after the night before and you haven't even been anywhere.

Milton Berle

You know you're knocking on when you get to the top of the stairs and can't remember what you went up for. So you go back downstairs to help you remember what you went upstairs for. You finally remember what you went upstairs for so up you go again but when you find it you have forgotten why you wanted it.

Millicent Kemp

When the Pope Starts Looking Young

You know you're getting older when the first thing you do after you're done eating is look for a place to lie down.

Louie Anderson

A young boy down the road tried to help me across the road this afternoon. I gave him a swift cuff round the ear. Only be a matter of time before they're forcing me on a day-trip to Eastbourne.

Victor Meldrew, One Foot in the Grave

You know you're getting old when you go on holiday and always pack a sweater.

Denis Norden

You're getting old when you stop loving snow and sweetcorn.

Susan H. Llewellyn

You know you're getting old when you and your partner wear matching sweaters.

Mark Schofield

I know I'm getting older because these days, before I leave in the morning, I have to ask myself, 'Did I remember to pluck my ears?'

Christopher Moore

When the Pope Starts Looking Young

You know you're getting old when you open the fridge door and can't remember if you're putting something in or taking something out.

Lottie Robson

You know you're getting old when your grown children get you as a present one of those stupid books about 'the joys of ageing'.

Garrison Keillor

You know you're getting old when you turn out the light for economic reasons instead of romantic ones.

Herbert J. Kavet

You know you're getting on when you start getting symptoms in the places you used to get urges.

Denis Norden

You know you're getting old when you don't notice the smell any more when the toast burns.

Ron Jowker

You know you're getting old when you're dashing through Marks and Spencer's, spot a pair of Dr Scholl's sandals, stop, and think, hmm, they look comfy.

Victoria Wood

When the Pope Starts Looking Young

You know you're getting old when you're no longer offered a puff of the latest perfume at the department store.

Rowena Kemp

You know you're getting old when your wife believes your excuses for getting home late.

Basil Ransome-Davies

You know you're old when your family talk about you in front of you. What are we going to do with Pop? We have company tonight.

Rodney Dangerfield

Being old is getting up in the middle of the night as often as George Clooney, but not for the same reason.

Mel Brooks

Twice-nightly Whiteley? Sometimes it's Thrice-nightly Whiteley. That man is a martyr to his bladder.

Kathyrn Apanowicz, partner of Richard Whiteley

You know you're getting old when you're interested in going home before you get where you're going.

Alan Mainwaring

A man knows he is growing old because he begins to look like his father.

Gabriel García Márquez

You know you're getting old when you start to like your mum and dad again. 'Yes, mum, I'd love to come caravanning to Tenby with you. No, I'll bring a packed lunch. I'm not paying café prices.'

Jeff Green

You know you're getting old when a four-letter word for something pleasurable two people can do in bed is R-E-A-D.

Denis Norden

You know you're getting old when you stoop to tie your shoelaces and wonder what else you can do while you're down there.

George Burns

You Know You're Getting Old When...

...the only thing you want for your birthday is not to be reminded of it.

You Know You're Getting Old When...

...'Happy Hour' turns out to be a nap.

...it takes you all night to do what you used to do all night.

...you sink your teeth into an apple and they stay there.

...your back goes out more often than you do.

...you can't get your rocking chair started.

...it feels like the morning after and you haven't been anywhere.

...you get winded playing chess.

...being a little hippie does not have the same meaning as it did in the 60s.

...everything either dries up or leaks.

...you go for a mammogram and you realise it is the only time someone will ever ask you to appear topless in a film.

...your wife gives up sex for Lent, and you don't know till the 4th of July.

All Anon

...you've lost all your marvels.

Merry Browne

...you walk into a record store and everything you like has been marked down to $1.99.

Jack Simmons

...all the names in your black book have M. D. after them.

Arnold Palmer

...the candles cost more than the cake.

George Burns

Old Age

At a church social, a little boy came up and asked me how old I was. I said, 'I'm 76.' 'And you're still alive?' he said.

Jack Wilson

Alive in the sense that he can't legally be buried.

Geoffrey Madan

—Smithers, what's my password?
—It's your age, sir.
—Excellent! [*four beeps are heard*]

Mr Burns and Smithers, The Simpsons

Old Age

—I'm a college professor. What did you think when I said I taught Hemingway?
—I thought you were old.

Miles Webber and Rose Martin, The Golden Girls

I'm so old that when I order a three-minute egg, they ask for the money up front.

Milton Berle

I'm so old I daren't even buy green bananas.

Bruce Forsyth

I'm at an age when if I drop a fiver in the collection plate, it's not a donation, it's an investment.

Ralph Layton

Anyone can get old. All you have to do is to live long enough.

Groucho Marx

How do you know when you're old? When you double your current age and realize you're not going to live that long.

Michael Leyden

I'm 59 and people call me middle-aged. How many 118-year-old men do you know?

Barry Cryer

Old age is like waiting in the departure lounge of life. Fortunately, we are in England and the train is bound to be late.

Milton Shulman

You are as young as your faith, as old as your doubt; as young as your self-confidence, as old as your fear; as young as your hope, as old as your despair.

Douglas MacArthur

I hope I never get so old I get religious.

Ingmar Bergman

Old age is not for sissies.

Bette Davis

I don't know how you feel about old age, but in my case I didn't even see it coming. It hit me from the rear.

Phyllis Diller

The ageing process is not gradual or gentle. It rushes up, pushes you over and runs off laughing. Dying is a matter of slapstick and pratfalls.

John Mortimer

Old Age

Old age is like underwear. It creeps up on you.

Lois L. Kaufman

Old age is the most unexpected of all things that happen to a man.

Leon Trotsky

A person is always startled when he hears himself called an old man for the first time.

Oliver Wendell Holmes

I do what I can to help the elderly; after all, I'm going to be old myself some day.

Lillian Carter, 76

The older I get, the older old is.

Tom Baker

To me, old age is always 15 years older than I am.

Bernard Baruch

I'm Too Young to be This Old

Slogan on a senior citizen's T-shirt

Inside yourself, you're still the same age as you were when you were 11. It's just that various bits keep dropping off.

John Mortimer

Old Age

I don't feel old. In fact I don't feel anything until noon. Then it's time for my nap.

Bob Hope

Old age is when you know all the answers, but nobody asks you the questions.

Laurence J. Peter

Old age is realizing you will never own all the dogs you wanted to.

Joe Gores

Old age is a time of life when the phone rings less often, but more ominously.

Edmund Volkart

Old is when your wife says, 'Let's go upstairs and make love,' and you answer, 'Honey, I can't do both.'

Red Buttons

Old age is a lot of crossed-off names in your address book.

Ronald Blythe

W. C. Fields has a profound respect for old age. Especially when it's bottled.

Gene Fowler

Old Age

Every age can be enchanting, provided you live within it.

Brigitte Bardot

Women never have young minds. They are born 3,000 years old.

Shelagh Delaney

There is no old age. There is, as there always was, just you.

Carol Matthau

Old age is like a plane flying through a storm. Once you are aboard there is nothing you can do about it. So one might as well accept it calmly, wisely.

Golda Meir

There's one more terrifying fact about old people: I'm going to be one soon.

P.J. O'Rourke

Old age isn't so bad when you consider the alternative.

Maurice Chevalier

Appearance

—Good afternoon, I'm Dorothy Zbornak.
—Geriatrics is two doors down on the left.

Dorothy Zbornak and Hospital Receptionist, Empty Nest

There is a saying, 'Youth is a gift of nature; age is a work of art.' If age is a work of art, the artist is one who belongs on the subway and not in the Louvre.

Bill Cosby

As I rose from my bath, I caught sight of myself in the mirror. I suddenly saw a great white sea monster emerging out of the water. This enormous subaquatic creature could not possibly be me, could it?

Julian Fellowes

I still think of myself as I was 25 years ago. Then I look in the mirror and see an old bastard and I realize it's me.

Dave Allen

Let us be grateful to the mirror for revealing to us our appearance only.

Samuel Butler

Appearance

It is 11 years since I have seen my figure in a mirror: the last reflection I saw there was so disagreeable I resolved to spare myself such mortification in the future, and shall continue that resolution to my life's end.

Lady Mary Wortley Montagu

Sometimes I catch a glimpse of my outward self reflected in a shop window and see my mother. That old woman can't be me!

Prue Phillipson

A while ago I asked John Clarke to give us a talk here at Knapely Women's Institute. Annie asked me to read it to you here tonight, and this is what he wrote: 'The flowers of Yorkshire are like the women of Yorkshire. Every stage of their growth has its own beauty, but the last phase is always the most glorious. Then very quickly they all go to seed.'

Chris, Calendar Girls

If you really want to annoy your glamorous, well-preserved 42-year-old auntie, say, 'I bet you were really pretty when you were young.'

Lily Savage

Twenty-four years ago, Madam, I was incredibly handsome. The remains of it are still visible through the rift of time. I was so handsome that women became spellbound when I came in view. In San Francisco, in rainy seasons, I was frequently mistaken for a cloudless day.

Mark Twain

After a certain number of years, our faces become our biographies.

Cynthia Ozick

Eric Sykes is about to be 79. He has the stretching, slowly inquiring, slightly dome-y head of one of those lovely, ancient sea turtles you see on wildlife programmes.

Deborah Ross

An old man looks permanent, as if he had been born an old man.

H. E. Bates

I have reached the age when I look just as good standing on my head as I do right-side up.

Frank Sullivan

Jesus! Look at my hands. Now really, I am too young for liver spots. Maybe I can merge them into a tan.

Diane, September

Appearance

I swear I'm ageing about as well as a beach-party movie.

Harvey Fierstein, Torch Song Trilogy

I beg your pardon, I didn't recognize you – I've changed a lot.

Oscar Wilde

Do I look older? Look at my face, sweetie? What do you see? You may lie, darling, I'm just looking for a response.

Edina Monsoon, Absolutely Fabulous

I've got enough crow's feet to start a bird sanctuary.

Kathy Lette

After a certain age, a woman should never leave the house.

Jennifer Jones

I've often thought that the ageing process could be slowed down if it had to work its way through Parliament.

Edwina Currie

First I was 'pretty'. Now I'm 'interesting – got character'. Soon I'll be 'handsome' and then, worst of all, I'll be 'remarkable for my age'.

Valerie Harper, Chapter Two

I didn't want to look my age, but I didn't want to act the age I wanted to look, either. I also wanted to grow old enough to understand that sentence.

Erma Bombeck

As long as a woman can look 10 years younger than her own daughter, she is perfectly satisfied.

Oscar Wilde

My looks had gone by the age of 7.

Dodie Smith

Walking past a building site on my way to the shops, I was wolf-whistled by a hunky construction worker on some scaffolding. I'm 63. It made my day.

Janet Lynn

You can be glamorous at any age. It is not the prerogative of the young. In fact, the self-confidence of experience is an added bonus.

Joan Collins

Sex appeal is 50 per cent what you've got and 50 per cent what people think you've got.

Sophia Loren

Appearance

Cut off my head and I am 13.

Coco Chanel, 60

Good cheekbones are the brassiere of old age.

Barbara de Portago

So much has been said and sung of beautiful young girls, why doesn't somebody wake up to the beauty of old women?

Harriet Beecher Stowe

No spring, nor summer beauty hath such grace,
As I have seen in one autumnal face.

John Donne, 'The Autumnal' Elegy

She had accomplished what, according to builders, is only possible to wood and stone of the very finest grain; she had weathered, as they call it, with beauty.

Ethel Smyth

I won't ever feel old, and I won't ever look old because I'm a cartoon – like Mickey Mouse.

Dolly Parton

I'm at that age when everything Mother Nature gave me, Father Time is taking away.

George Burns

Appearance

When I go upstairs my buttocks applaud me and my knees sound like potato chips.

Joan Rivers

Women are not forgiven for ageing. Robert Redford's 'lines of distinction' are my 'old-age wrinkles'.

Jane Fonda

There are new lines on my face. I look like a brand-new, steel-belted radial tyre.

Diana Barrie, California Suite

If God had to give a woman wrinkles He might at least have put them on the soles of her feet.

Ninon de Lenclos

One thing to be said for wrinkles – at least they don't hurt.

Betty Smith

Keep looking at my eyes, dahling. My arse is like an accordion.

Tallulah Bankhead

It's hard to be devil-may-care when there are pleats in your derrière.

Judith Viorst

Appearance

I said to my husband, my boobs have gone, my stomach's gone, say something nice about my legs. He said, 'Blue goes with everything.'

Joan Rivers

Mick Jagger told me the wrinkles on his face were laughter lines, but nothing is that funny.

George Melly

When I looked at the wrinkled skin on W. H. Auden's face, I kept wondering, what must his balls look like?

David Hockney

I'm not really wrinkled. I just took a nap on a chenille bedspread.

Phyllis Diller

—I haven't got bad boobs for a woman of my age.
—Behave, Barbara. They're like bloody spaniels' ears.

Barbara and Jim Royle, The Royle Family

I have everything I had 20 years ago, only now it's six inches lower.

Gypsy Rose Lee

Whenever I see some floozy in a boob tube I scream, 'Listen, honey, even the Roman Empire fell, and those things will, too.'

Phyllis Diller

Thirty years ago I got a tattoo of the yellow rose of Texas and green leaf, right above my heart. But with age comes sagging, and my yellow rose of Texas is now down to my waist and looks like a picture of Tony Bennett with liver disease and an elf hat.

Sally Jackson

I no longer have upper arms. I have wing-span.

Bette Midler

You are rapidly approaching the age when your body, whether it embarrasses you or not, begins to embarrass other people.

Alan Bennett, Getting On

Fat people don't seem to age as much as thin people, not when you get close up and inspect the damage.

Hunter Davies

After 40 a woman has to choose between losing her figure or her face. My advice is to keep your face, and stay sitting down.

Barbara Cartland

Appearance

Nature gives you the face you have at 20. Life shapes the face you have at 30. But at 50 you get the face you deserve.

Coco Chanel

There are people who are beautiful in dilapidation, like houses that were hideous when new.

Logan Pearsall Smith

Like all ruins, I look best by moonlight. Give me a sprig of ivy and an owl under my arm and Tintern Abbey would not be in it with me.

W. S. Gilbert

The paint and plaster may be peeling and cracking on the outside but that doesn't matter if the rooms inside are warm and cosy.

Anon

How pleasant is the day when we give up striving to be young – or slender.

William James

Most women are not as young as they are painted.

Max Beerbohm

My face looks like a wedding cake left out in the rain.

W. H. Auden

As we get older, our bodies get shorter and our anecdotes get longer.

Robert Quillen

I guess I look like a rock quarry that someone has dynamited.

Charles Bronson

Like a lot of fellows around here, I have a furniture problem. My chest has fallen into my drawers.

Billy Casper

If a woman tells you she's 20 and looks 16, she's 12. If she tells you she's 26 and looks 26, she's damn near 40.

Chris Rock

Robert Redford used to be such a handsome man and now look at him: everything has dropped, expanded and turned a funny colour.

George Best

The outer passes away; the innermost is the same yesterday, today, and forever.

Thomas Carlyle

Appearance

Many of my contemporaries have terrible feet, deformed by bunions, permanent corns and layers of dead skin like rock strata.

Sue Townsend

The problem with beauty is that it's like being born rich and getting poorer.

Joan Collins

Time may be a great healer, but it's a lousy beautician.

Lucille S. Harper

I ain't what I used to be, but who the hell is?

Dizzy Dean

I spent seven hours in a beauty shop – and that was just for the estimate.

Phyllis Diller

Take my photograph? You might as well use a picture of a relief map of Ireland!

Nancy Astor

I have a face like the behind of an elephant.

Charles Laughton

Appearance

Naked, I had a body that invited burial.

Spike Milligan

One day you look in the mirror and you realise that the face you are shaving is your father's.

Robert Harris

Some people, no matter how old they get, never lose their beauty – they merely move it from their faces into their hearts.

Martin Buxbaum

When I look in the mirror I don't see a rock star any more. I see a little balding old guy who looks like someone's uncle.

Pete Townshend

Wrinkles should merely indicate where smiles have been.

Mark Twain

You know you're getting fat when you can pinch an inch on your forehead.

John Mendoza

People say that age is just a state of mind. I say it's more about the state of your body.

Geoffrey Parfitt

Appearance

Time wounds all heels.

Groucho Marx

I have a face that is a cross between two pounds of halibut and an explosion in an old clothes closet.

David Niven

I look just like the girl next door … if you happen to live next to an amusement park.

Dolly Parton

Old age is when the liver spots show through your gloves.

Phyllis Diller

A man's as old as he's feeling. A woman as old as she looks.

Mortimer Collins

The excesses of our youth are cheques written against our age and they are payable with interest 30 years later.

Charles Caleb Colton

Looking 50 is great – if you're 60.

Joan Rivers

At age 50, everyone has the face he deserves.

George Orwell

At 50, you have the choice of keeping your face or your figure and it's much better to keep your face.

Barbara Cartland

Anatomically speaking, a bust is here today and gone tomorrow.

Isobel Barnett

He must have had a magnificent build before his stomach went in for a career of its own.

Margaret Halsey

Muscles come and go; flab lasts.

Bill Vaughan

You can only perceive real beauty in a person as they get older.

Anouk Aimée

Men become much more attractive when they start looking older. But it doesn't do much for women, though we do have an advantage: make-up.

Bette Davis

Appearance

Intellectual blemishes, like facial ones, grow more prominent with age.

François de La Rochefoucauld

I'd like to change my butt. It hangs a little too long. God forbid what it will look like when I'm older. It will probably be dragging along on the ground behind me.

Teri Hatcher

I'm tired of all this nonsense about beauty being only skin-deep. That's deep enough. What do you want – an adorable pancreas?

Jean Kerr

I don't believe make-up and the right hairstyle alone can make a woman beautiful. The most radiant woman in the room is the one full of life and experience.

Sharon Stone

If you want to look young and thin, hang around old fat people.

Jim Eason

Thank God for beauty products because at least they give you hope. Even if they do nothing for you, you can sort of slam the box to your forehead and think it's helping. And it has to be expensive stuff because if it's cheap stuff, it won't work. I'm not interested in cheap stuff. I don't care if it's all packaging, that's fine by me. Just as long as it sells me a dream.

Nina Myskow, Grumpy Old Women

It's time we stopped worrying about losing our looks and started celebrating the gifts of age: I feel yummier than ever.

Sela Ward

I am sitting here thinking how nice it is that wrinkles don't hurt.

Anon

I don't think age is an ugly process. I think age is a beautiful thing. I love wrinkles. I don't like falling down. If I just wrinkle, I may not touch. If I fall down, I'll lift up.

Linda Evangelista

A beautiful lady is an accident of nature. A beautiful old lady is a work of art.

Louis Nizer

When you have loved as she has loved, you grow old beautifully.

W. Somerset Maugham

Appearance

Midlife has hit you when you stand naked in front of a mirror and can see your rear end without turning around!

Anon

The older I get, the more I feel almost beautiful.

Sharon Olds

I guess I don't so much mind being old, as I mind being fat and old.

Peter Gabriel

You can take no credit for beauty at 16. But if you are beautiful at 60, it will be your own soul's doing.

Marie Stopes

It really costs me a lot emotionally to watch myself on-screen. I think of myself, and feel like I'm quite young, and then I look at this old man with the baggy chins and the tired eyes and the receding hairline and all that.

Gene Hackman

Midlife is when the growth of the hair on our legs slows down. This gives us plenty of time to care for our newly acquired moustache.

Anon

Middle age is when your wife tells you to pull in your stomach, and you already have.

Jack Barry

I am going to carry on colouring my hair, wearing diamonds and painting my nails until the day I die.

Jenni Murray

Liza Minnelli looks like a very old 13.

Jonathan Ross

Midlife women no longer have upper arms, we have wing-spans. We are no longer women in sleeveless shirts; we are flying squirrels in drag.

Anon

I think that the longer I look good, the better gay men feel.

Cher

It's okay to be fat. So you're fat. Just be fat and shut up about it.

Roseanne Barr

It's simple: if it jiggles, it's fat.

Arnold Schwarzenegger

Appearance

The older you get, the tougher it is to lose weight, because by then your body and your fat are really good friends.

Anon

If I had been around when Rubens was painting, I would have been revered as a fabulous model. Kate Moss? Well, she would have been the paintbrush.

Dawn French

I'm going to have wrinkles really soon.

Cher

Character contributes to beauty. It fortifies a woman as her youth fades.

Jacqueline Bisset

In middle life, the human back is spoiling for a technical knockout and will use the flimsiest excuse, even a sneeze, to fall apart.

Elwyn Brooks White

Brilliantly lit from stem to stern, she looked like a sagging birthday cake.

Walter Lord

Even with all my wrinkles! I am beautiful!

Edward Everett Hale

Wear a smile and have friends; wear a scowl and have wrinkles.

George Eliot

Well, her face was so wrinkled it looked like seven miles of bad road.

W. C. Fields

Folding Back the Years

COSMETIC SURGERY

I want to grow old without face-lifts. I want to have the courage to be loyal to the face I have made.

Marilyn Monroe

I'd make plastic surgery compulsory for every woman over 40.

Simon Cowell

My husband said 'show me your boobs' and I had to pull up my skirt … so it was time to get them done!

Dolly Parton

Folding Back the Years

Please don't retouch my wrinkles. It took me so long to earn them.

Anna Magnani

A plastic surgeon's office is the only place where no one gets offended when you pick your nose.

MAD Magazine

I don't suggest that her face has been lifted, but there's a possibility that her body has been lowered.

Clive James

The only parts left of my original body are my elbows.

Phyllis Diller

Look at Cher. One more face-lift and she'll be wearing a beard.

Jennifer Saunders

Sylvester Stallone's mother's plastic surgery looks so bad it could have been bought through a mail-order catalogue.

Graham Norton

I don't need plastic surgery. I need Lourdes.

Paul O'Grady

Why fear terrorists? With treatments like botox, women are waging germ warfare on themselves at £250 a pop.

Kathy Lette

If anybody says their face-lift doesn't hurt, they're lying. It was like I'd spent the night with an axe murderer.

Sharon Osbourne

I was going to have cosmetic surgery until I noticed that the doctor's office was full of portraits by Picasso.

Rita Rudner

Teething Troubles

I had very good dentures once. Some magnificent gold work. It's the only form of jewellery a man can wear that women fully appreciate.

Graham Greene

Dentures: Two rows of artificial ivories that may be removed periodically to frighten one's grandchildren or provide accompaniment to Spanish music.

Anon

Teething Troubles

It is after you have lost your teeth that you can afford to buy steaks.

Pierre Auguste Renoir

We idolised the Beatles, except for those of us who idolised the Rolling Stones, who in those days still had many of their original teeth.

Dave Barry

I've gotten to the age where I need my false teeth and hearing aid before I can ask where I left my glasses.

Anon

I don't have false teeth. Do you think I'd buy teeth like these?

Carol Burnett

Every tooth in a man's head is more valuable than a diamond.

Miguel de Cervantes

I like my bifocals,
my dentures fit me fine,
my hearing aid is perfect,
but Lord I miss my mind!

Anon

She had so many gold teeth … she used to have to sleep with her head in a safe.

W.C. Fields

Now Bart, since you broke Grandpa's teeth, he gets to break yours.

Homer Simpson, The Simpsons

The good news about mid-life is that the glass is still half-full. Of course, the bad news is that it won't be long before your teeth are floating in it.

Anon

Ribs, great … why don't you just kick the dentures out of my mouth?

Sophia Petrillo, The Golden Girls

I swear, if Colgate comes out with one more type of toothpaste … I just want clean teeth; that's all I want. I don't want the tartar and I don't want the cavities. And I want white teeth. How come I have to choose? And then they have the 'Colgate Total' that supposedly has everything in there. I don't believe that for one second. If it's all in the one, how come they make all the others? Who's going: 'I don't mind the tartar so much'?

Ellen DeGeneres

God gives nuts to those with no teeth.

Anon

Dress

Dorothy, was Sophia naked just now or does her dress really need ironing?

Rose Nylund, The Golden Girls

Men in the uniform of Wall Street retirement: black Chesterfield coat, rimless glasses and *The Times* folded to the obituary page.

Jimmy Breslin

Inspired by the line in Jenny Joseph's poem 'Warning' that vows, 'When I am an old woman, I shall wear purple, with a red hat that doesn't go', I started 'The Red Hat Society'. It's for women who want to grow old playfully.

Sue Ellen Cooper

Never wear grey. Wearing grey makes one feel grey. I was shown round Tutankhamun's tomb in the 1920s. I saw all this wonderful pink on the walls and the artefacts. I was so impressed that I vowed to wear it for the rest of my life.

Barbara Cartland

—Dorothy, do you think I'm dressed okay for the dog races?
—That depends – are you competing?

Blanche Devereaux and Sophia Petrillo, The Golden Girls

My mother buys me those big granny panties, three in a pack. You can use them for a car cover.

Monique Marvez

Caesar had his toga, Adam had his leaf, but when I wear a thong it gives my piles such grief.

Sandra Mayhew

My dad's trousers kept creeping up on him. By the time he was 65, he was just a pair of pants and a head.

Jeff Altman

I have never seen an old person in a new bathing suit in my life. I don't know where they get their bathing suits, but my father has bathing suits from other centuries. If I forget mine, he always wants me to wear his.

Jerry Seinfeld

I'm a child of the Sixties. I still wear jeans and yes, my bum looks big in them but then my bum looked big in 1965.

Julia Richardson

Dress

I can see nothing wrong with 40-, 50-, or 60-year-old men dressing and acting like teenagers. I'm an elderly man of 44 and, after a few miserable years of being sensible, I do it all the time.

Jeremy Clarkson

A sign your best years are behind you is when you slip into your first pair of slippers. They smack of smugness and a grisly domesticity.

Piers Hernu

Roll carpet slippers in breadcrumbs, bake until golden brown, then tell friends you're wearing Findus Crispy Pancakes.

H. Lloyd, Top Tip, Viz

At 50, confine your piercings to sardine cans.

Joan Rivers

—Now, if you'll excuse me, I'm going to slip into something that will make me look my best.
—May I suggest a time machine?

Blanche Devereaux and Sophia Petrillo, The Golden Girls

After 50 a man discovers he does not need more than one suit.

Clifton Fadiman

Being home on a Friday night with the old man, an Indian take-away and a nice bottle of wine, and there's something on the telly – oh, I like that. I'm in my dressing gown, I mean it's not a weird dressing gown, it's not one of those quilted old lady ones. It's Cath Kidston. It's quite a funky dressing gown … don't get me wrong. I'm not that old.

Jenny Eclair, Grumpy Old Women

If women dressed for men, the stores wouldn't sell much – just an occasional sun visor.

Groucho Marx

Underwear makes me uncomfortable and besides, my parts have to breathe.

Jean Harlow

Trying on pants is one of the most humiliating things a man can suffer that doesn't involve a woman.

Larry David

You'd be surprised how much it costs to look this cheap.

Dolly Parton

I am 56 years old, an age when many women tend not to be noticed as we plod about in our extra-wide, midi-heeled sensible shoes.

Sue Townsend

Dress

You can say what you like about long dresses, but they cover a multitude of shins.

Mae West

She looked as if she had been poured into her clothes and had forgotten to say 'when'.

P. G. Wodehouse

Brevity is the soul of lingerie.

Dorothy Parker

Dress simply. If you wear a dinner jacket, don't wear anything else on it … like lunch or dinner.

George Burns

Nothing goes out of fashion sooner than a long dress with a very low neck.

Coco Chanel

Fashion is what you adopt when you don't know who you are.

Quentin Crisp

The only man I know who behaves sensibly is my tailor; he takes my measurements anew each time he sees me. The rest go on with their old measurements and expect me to fit them.

George Bernard Shaw

If God had meant us to walk around naked, he would never have invented the wicker chair.

Erma Bombeck

Gloves complete a look. That's my belief. Who cares if I'm right or wrong? I had a mother who encouraged me to go with impulses. And I have, and it's led to some insanely ridiculous outfits, but I like it that way.

Diane Keaton

I wouldn't say I invented tacky, but I definitely brought it to its present high popularity.

Bette Midler

How on earth did Gandhi manage to walk so far in flip-flops? I can't last 10 minutes in mine.

Mrs Merton

I don't think I would've worn thongs even when I was young and trying very hard. No, that's ridiculous. You might as well go without knickers at all.

Annette Crosbie, Grumpy Old Women

And you know, the baby boomers are getting older, and those off-the-rack clothes are just not fitting right any longer, and so, tailor-made suits are coming back into fashion.

Amy Irving

Dress

I base my fashion taste on what doesn't itch.

Gilda Radner

Now that I'm old [clothes shopping] has become entirely frustrating because there is nothing for me to wear in the shops. Nothing. I mean, I'm not going to wear hipster pants, am I? If I wear hipster pants and I sit down, I'll shoot out the back of them. It's not on.

Germaine Greer, Grumpy Old Women

Show me a man with both feet on the ground and I'll show you a man who can't get his pants on.

Joe E. Lewis

Tell me the history of that frock, Janet. It's obviously an old favourite. You were wise to remove the curtain rings. I love that fabric. You were lucky to find so much of it.

Dame Edna Everage

Once you can accept the universe as matter expanding into nothing that is something, wearing stripes with plaid comes easy.

Albert Einstein

Women's clothes: never wear anything that panics the cat.

P.J. O'Rourke

Some women hold up dresses that are so ugly and they always say the same thing: 'This looks much better on.' On what? On fire?

Marsha Warfield

Hilary: One of the few lessons I have learned in life is that there is invariably something odd about women who wear ankle socks.

Alan Bennett, The Old Country

Fashion is a form of ugliness so intolerable that we have to alter it every six months.

Oscar Wilde

I grow old … I grow old … I shall wear the bottoms of my trousers rolled.

T. S. Eliot

I wouldn't say her bathing suit was skimpy, but I've seen more cotton in the top of an aspirin bottle.

Henny Youngman

Dress

Denise: Dad, stop fiddling with yerself.
Jim: I'm not fiddling with meself. I paid a quid for these underpants and I've got 50 pence stuck up me arse.

Denise and Jim Royle, The Royle Family

I know what Victoria's Secret is. The secret is that nobody older than 30 can fit into their stuff.

Sima Jacobson

A hat should be taken off when you greet a lady and left off for the rest of your life. Nothing looks more stupid than a hat.

P. J. O'Rourke

Though I am grateful for the blessings of wealth, it hasn't changed who I am. My feet are still on the ground. I'm just wearing better shoes.

Oprah Winfrey

I never cared for fashion much: amusing little seams and witty little pleats. It was the girls I liked.

David Bailey

Hair Today, Gone Tomorrow

I found my first grey hair today. On my chest.

Wendy Liebman

A wonderful woman, my grandmother – 86 years old and not a single grey hair on her head. She's completely bald.

Les Dawson

When men get grey hair, they look distinguished. When women get grey hair, they look old. When women get breasts, they look sexy. When men get breasts, they look old.

Dick Solomon

Grey-haired men look 'distinguished'? Surely the word is 'extinguished'.

Julie Burchill

I'm so grey, I look like I'm gonna rain sometimes. And my pubic hair is going grey. In a certain light you'd swear it was Stewart Granger down there.

Billy Connolly

I used to think I'd like less grey hair. Now I'd like more of it.

Richie Benaud

Hair Today, Gone Tomorrow

I knew I was going bald when it was taking longer and longer to wash my face.

Harry Hill

The method preferred by most balding men for making themselves look silly is called the 'comb-over', which is when the man grows the hair on one side of his head very long and combs it across the bald area, creating an effect that looks from the top like an egg in the grasp of a large tropical spider.

Dave Barry

Men going bald is Nature's way of stopping them having any more crap hairstyles.

Tony, Men Behaving Badly

Peter Stringfellow's hairstyle is older than some of his girlfriends.

Paul Merton

There's one good thing about being bald: it's neat.

Milton Berle

The most delightful advantage of being bald – one can hear snowflakes.

R.G. Daniels

Hair Today, Gone Tomorrow

I love bald men. Just because you've lost your fuzz doesn't mean you ain't a peach.

Dolly Parton

Over the years, I've tried a variety of ways to regain my hair. I had shots of oestrogen in my scalp. I didn't grow any hair – but I went up a cup size.

Tony Kornheiser

—Do you think she's wearing a wig?
—Yes, definitely, but it's a very good one. You'd never guess.

Two old ladies overheard on a bus

People ask me how long it takes to do my hair. I don't know, I'm never there.

Dolly Parton

The hair is real. It's the head that's fake.

Steve Allen

His toupee makes him look 20 years sillier.

Bill Dana

If that thing had legs it'd be a rat.

Martin Kemp

Hair Today, Gone Tomorrow

Things For Guys to Consider Before Buying a Hairpiece: Will it appreciate in value? Is it possible a hairpiece will make me look too good? Will I be able to handle all the women? Have I explored all my comb-over options?

David Letterman

—Hi, Stan. Where's your hair?
—Oh damn, I should have never let the sun-roof down.

Rose Nylund and Stan Zbornak, The Golden Girls

Wig wearers! Secure your toupee in high winds by wearing a brightly coloured party hat with elasticated chin strap. Carry a balloon and a bottle of wine, and you'll pass off as an innocent party-goer.

F. Fine-Fare, Top Tip, Viz

By common consent, grey hairs are a crown of glory: the only object of respect that can never excite envy.

George Bancroft

There is only one cure for grey hair. It was invented by a Frenchman. It is called the guillotine.

P. G. Wodehouse

Hair Today, Gone Tomorrow

It is not by the grey of the hair that one knows the age of the heart.

Edward Bulwer-Lytton

It seems no more than right that men should seize time by the forelock, for the rude old fellow, sooner or later, pulls all their hair out.

George Dennison Prentice

There is more felicity on the far side of baldness than young men can possibly imagine.

Logan Pearsall Smith

Inflation is when you pay $15 for the $10 haircut you used to get for five dollars when you had hair.

Sam Ewing

Grey hair is God's graffiti.

Bill Cosby

I'm entering the 'metallic years'; silver in my hair, gold in my teeth and lead in my bottom!

Anon

André Gide was very bald with the general look of an elderly fallen angel travelling incognito.

Peter Quennell

Hair Today, Gone Tomorrow

On the bright side of life you will probably save a lot on shampoo when getting old and bald, and no longer have to suffer from thwarted and long-gone ambitions.

T. Kinnes

After watching Cary Grant on a television broadcast, his mother, then in her 90s, reprimanded him for letting his hair get so grey. 'It doesn't bother me,' the actor replied carelessly. 'Maybe not,' said his mother, 'but it bothers *me*. It makes me seem so old.'

Anon

The best thing about being bald is when her folks come home; all you have to do is straighten your tie.

Milton Berle

He wore his baldness like an expensive hat.

Gloria Swanson

My husband was bending over to tie my three-year-old's shoes. That's when I noticed my son Ben staring at my husband's head. He gently touched the slightly thinning spot of hair and said in a concerned voice, 'Daddy, you have a hole in your head. Does it hurt?' After a pause, I heard my husband's murmured reply, 'Not physically.'

Reader's Digest

Hair Today, Gone Tomorrow

Women love a self-confident bald man.

Larry David

I'm not really bald. I just have a very wide parting.

Anon

The tenderest spot in a man's make-up is sometimes the bald spot on top of his head.

Helen Rowland

Violet will be a good colour for hair at just about the same time that brunette becomes a good colour for flowers.

Fran Lebowitz

The simple truth is that balding African-American men look cool when they shave their heads, whereas balding white men look like giant thumbs.

Dave Barry

Grey hairs are signs of wisdom if you hold your tongue.
Speak and they are but hairs, as in the young.

Anon

We're all born bald, baby.

Telly Savalas

Hair Today, Gone Tomorrow

I feel old when I see mousse in my opponent's hair.

Andre Agassi

I'm not bald … I'm just taller than my hair.

Clive Anderson

I know body hair bothers some women, but a lot of men like a fluffy partner.

Dame Edna Everage

You can always tell where Diana Ross has been by the hair that's left behind!

Diana Ross

The secret of my success is my hairspray.

Richard Gere

A man is usually bald four or five years before he knows it.

Ed Howe

The worst thing a man can do is go bald. Never let yourself go bald.

Donald Trump

He's the kind of guy that, when he dies, he's going up to heaven and give God a bad time for making him bald.

Marlon Brando, on Frank Sinatra

It's a question that I find like asking somebody, 'Did you have a breast implant?' or 'When did you get your lobotomy?

William Shatner, when asked if he wore a hairpiece

My hairdresser actually spends more time digging hair out of my ears than off the top or back of my head.

Des Lynam, Grumpy Old Men

When others kid me about being bald, I simply tell them that the way I figure it, the good Lord only gave men so many hormones, and if others want to waste theirs on growing hair, that's up to them.

John Glenn

A hair in the head is worth two in the brush.

Don Herold

Eat, Drink and Be Merry ...

As I get older, I'm trying to eat healthy. I've got Gordon Ramsay's new cookbook, *Take Two Eggs and Fuck Off.*

Jack Dee

Eat, Drink and Be Merry ...

Joan Collins says you are what you eat. She reached this conclusion following experiences in the swinging sixties and is very careful about what she puts in her mouth these days.

Mrs Merton

I'm at the age when food has taken the place of sex in my life. In fact, I've just had a mirror put over my kitchen table.

Rodney Dangerfield

Gin is a dangerous drink. It's clear and innocuous-looking. You also have to be 45, female and sitting on the stairs.

Dylan Moran

I'll tell you what I haven't seen for a long time: my testicles.

John Sparkes

I've gained a few pounds around the middle. The only lower-body garments I own that still fit me comfortably are towels.

Dave Barry

I don't have a beer belly. It's a Burgundy belly and it cost me a lot of money.

Charles Clarke

You can only hold your stomach in for so many years.

Burt Reynolds

Weighing scales are usually accurate, but never tactful.

Bill Cosby

I had to go to the doctor's last week. He told me to take all my clothes off. Then he said, 'You'll have to diet.' I said, 'What colour?'

Ken Dodd

I'm on a new diet – Viagra and prune juice. I don't know if I'm coming or going.

Rodney Dangerfield

Why is it all the things I like eating have been proven to cause tumours in white mice?

Robert Benchley

Welcome to the Wonderful World of 70: The Oat Bran Years.

Denis Norden

You do live longer with bran, but you spend the last 15 years on the toilet.

Alan King

Eat, Drink and Be Merry ...

Life expectancy would grow by leaps and bounds if green vegetables smelled as good as bacon.

Doug Larson

Cabbage she serves me. In ten minutes I could be sky-writing.

Sophia Petrillo, The Golden Girls

I don't eat health foods. At my age I need all the preservative I can get.

George Burns

Age does not diminish the extreme disappointment of having a scoop of ice cream fall from the cone.

Jim Freiberg

Part of the secret of success in life is to eat what you like and let the food fight it out inside.

Mark Twain

Nobody's last words have ever been, 'I wish I'd eaten more rice cakes.'

Amy Krouse Rosenthal

When you get to 52, food becomes more important than sex.

Prue Leith

Everything I eat has been proved by some doctor or other to be a deadly poison, and everything I don't eat has been proved to be indispensable for life. But I go marching on.

George Bernard Shaw

I've decided to make Granny Moon's Sheep's Head Soup. Don't worry, the name's a bit misleading. It's actually more of a stew.

Daphne Moon, Frasier

When men reach their 60s and retire they go to pieces. Women just go right on cooking.

Gail Sheehy

I refuse to spend my life worrying about what I eat. There is no pleasure worth forgoing just for an extra three years in the geriatric ward.

John Mortimer

I don't like food that's too carefully arranged; it makes me think that the chef is spending too much time arranging and not enough time cooking. If I wanted a picture I'd buy a painting.

Andy Rooney

I just love Chinese food. My favourite dish is number 27.

Clement Attlee

Eat, Drink and Be Merry...

My friend, Lily, can recognise 157 different cheeses just by looking at the labels.

Mrs Merton

Once, during prohibition, I was forced to live for days on nothing but food and water.

W. C. Fields

My doctor told me to stop having intimate dinners for four – unless there are three other people.

Orson Welles

A fruit is a vegetable with looks and money. Plus, if you let fruit rot, it turns into wine, something Brussels sprouts never do.

P.J. O'Rourke

I am a bit of a dictator when it comes to mealtimes. They have to eat their vegetables. They kick and scream to start with but if you persist they will eventually come round to your way of thinking. Now, a Brussels sprout is quite welcome in the family.

Antony Worrall Thompson

The English contribution to world cuisine – the chip.

John Cleese

It is inhumane, in my opinion, to force people who have a genuine medical need for coffee to wait in line behind people who apparently view it as some kind of recreational activity.

Dave Barry

Another teatime, another day older.

Jethro Tull

The funny thing about Thanksgiving, or any huge meal, is that you spend 12 hours shopping for it and then chopping and cooking and braising and blanching. Then it takes 20 minutes to eat it and everybody sort of sits around in a food coma, and then it takes four hours to clean it up.

Ted Allen

A wasp in an ice cube? What next? Dog turd on a cocktail stick?

Victor Meldrew

I will not eat oysters. I want my food dead. Not sick, not wounded, dead.

Woody Allen

Coffee in England always tastes like a chemistry experiment.

Agatha Christie

Ageing is when you hear 'snap, crackle, pop' before you get to breakfast.

Anon

It was a bold man who first swallowed an oyster.

Jonathan Swift

I don't cook any more. No one in their right mind does. People complain that young people no longer know how to, but I say, good. No one weaves their own cloth these days, either.

Shirley Conran

Kissing don't last; cookery do!

George Meredith

Cooking is like love. It should be entered into with abandon or not at all.

Harriet Van Horne

It's difficult to think anything but pleasant thoughts while eating a home-grown tomato.

Lewis Grizzard

High-tech tomatoes. Mysterious milk. Supersquash. Are we supposed to eat this stuff? Or is it going to eat us?

Annita Manning

I would like to find a stew that will give me heartburn immediately, instead of at three o'clock in the morning.

John Barrymore

Ask not what you can do for your country. Ask what's for lunch.

Orson Welles

One of the very nicest things about life is the way we must regularly stop whatever it is we are doing and devote our attention to eating.

Luciano Pavarotti and William Wright,
Pavarotti, My Own Story

What I say is that, if a man really likes potatoes, he must be a pretty decent sort of fellow.

A. A. Milne

I come from a family where gravy is considered a beverage.

Erma Bombeck

My idea of heaven is eating *pâté de foie gras* to the sound of trumpets.

Sydney Smith

Spaghetti can be eaten most successfully if you inhale it like a vacuum cleaner.

Sophia Loren

The only time to eat diet food is while you're waiting for the steak to cook.

Julia Child

People say fish is good for a diet. But fish should never be cooked in butter. Fish should be cooked in its natural oils – Texaco, Mobil, Exxon…

Rodney Dangerfield

Exercise

You gotta stay in shape. My grandmother started walking five miles a day when she was 60. She's 97 today and we don't know where the hell she is.

Ellen DeGeneres

I get up at 7am each day to do my exercises – after I have first put on my make-up. After all, La Loren is always La Loren.

Sophia Loren, 70

I exercise every morning without fail. Up, down! Up, down! And then the other eyelid.

Phyllis Diller

I swim a lot. It's either that or buy a new golf ball.

Bob Hope

I keep fit. Every morning, I do 100 laps of an Olympic-sized swimming pool – in a small motor launch.

Peter Cook

Police in Norway stopped Sigrid Krohn de Lange running down the street in Bergen because they thought that she had escaped from a nursing home. The 94-year-old jogger was out getting fit.

The Irish Independent

My doctor recently told me that jogging could add years to my life. I think he was right. I feel 10 years older already.

Milton Berle

The only reason I would take up jogging is so I could hear heavy breathing again.

Erma Bombeck

Exercise

Go jogging? What, and get hit by a meteor?

Robert Benchley

The doctor asked me if I ever got breathless after exercise. I said no, never, because I never exercise.

John Mortimer

I am pushing 60. That is enough exercise for me.

Mark Twain

To get back my youth, I would do anything in the world, except take exercise, get up early, or be respectable.

Oscar Wilde

Whenever I get the urge to exercise, I lie down until the feeling passes away.

Robert M. Hutchins

People are so busy lengthening their lives with exercise that they have no time to live them.

Jonathan Miller

Health nuts are going to feel stupid someday, lying in hospitals dying of nothing.

Redd Foxx

Exercise

I don't exercise. If God wanted me to bend over, he'd have put diamonds on the floor.

Joan Rivers

I get my exercise running to the funerals of my friends who exercise.

Barry Gray

I consider exercise vulgar. It makes people smell.

Alec Yuill Thornton

To resist the frigidity of old age, one must combine the body, the mind, and the heart. And to keep these in parallel vigour one must exercise, study, and love.

Alan Bleasdale

Once I realised how expensive funerals are, I began to exercise and watch my diet.

Thomas Sowell

If God wanted me to touch my toes, he would have put them on my knees.

Roseanne Barr

I get my exercise acting as a pallbearer to my friends who exercise.

Chauncey Depew

Exercise

Exercise is bunk. If you are healthy you don't need it. If you are sick you shouldn't take it.

Henry Ford

I like long walks, especially when they are taken by people who annoy me.

Fred Allen

My idea of exercise is a good brisk sit down.

Phyllis Diller

Jogging is very beneficial. It's good for your legs and your feet. It's also very good for the ground. It makes it feel needed.

Charles M. Schulz

Jogging is for people who aren't intelligent enough to watch television.

Victoria Wood

In the gym, I only wear black and diamonds.

Donatella Versace

You know you're into middle age when first you realise that caution is the only thing you care to exercise.

Charles Ghigna

Exercise

The trouble with jogging is that by the time you realise you're not in shape for it, it's too far to walk back.

Franklin P. Jones

I often take exercise. Only yesterday I had breakfast in bed.

Oscar Wilde

I bought all those celebrity exercise videos. I love to sit and eat cookies and watch them.

Dolly Parton

I have a punishing workout regimen. Every day I do three minutes on a treadmill, then I lie down, drink a glass of vodka and smoke a cigarette.

Anthony Hopkins

I've exercised with women so thin that buzzards followed them to their cars.

Erma Bombeck

I diet every day of my life. After 40 you've got to.

Kim Cattrall

Passing the vodka bottle. And playing the guitar.

Keith Richards, on how he keeps fit

I do try and keep fit, but it's a half-hearted battle. I'll go for a jog once a fortnight and then feel ill for two days afterwards. And now and again I'll join a health club, but the trauma of filling in the form and having my photo taken for the membership card usually puts me off going for about 12 months. But I'm still optimistic that one day I'll be offered a guest role in *Baywatch*.

Steve Coogan

The first time I see a jogger smiling, I'll consider it.

Joan Rivers

Sometimes I run around Regent's Park and go to the gym. I can manage about an hour, but stop for a cigarette every so often.

Julian Clary

You know you've reached middle age when your weightlifting consists of merely standing up.

Bob Hope

Showbiz and Hollywood

I am in an industry where they eat their elders.

Dale Winton

Showbiz and Hollywood

In Los Angeles, by the time you're 35, you're older than most of the buildings.

Delia Ephron

Actress years seem like dog years and that makes me about 266.

Sharon Stone

I can't think of anything grimmer than being an ageing actress – God! It's worse than being an ageing homosexual.

Candice Bergen

You have to be born a sex symbol. You don't become one. If you're born with it, you'll have it even when you're 100 years old.

Sophia Loren

In Hollywood, great-grandmothers dread growing old.

Phyllis Batelli

Oscar time is my busiest season. I'm like an accountant during the tax season.

Richard Fleming, Beverly Hills plastic surgeon

Showbiz and Hollywood

Arnold Schwarzenegger is getting old. He's changed his catchphrase from 'I'll be back' to 'Oh, my back'.

David Letterman

—You give your age here as 40. I happen to know that you are at least 50.
—Oh no, no, no. I absolutely refuse to count the last 10 years in Hollywood as part of my life.

Reporter and William Meiklejohn

Adam Faith is only 42, but Terry Nelhams is 62.

Adam Faith

I did not expect an honorary Oscar – well, actually, I did. But not for another 25 years.

Federico Fellini

Awards are like haemorrhoids: in the end every asshole gets one.

Frederic Raphael

That so many people respond to me is fabulous. It's like having a kind of Alzheimer's disease where everyone knows you and you don't know anyone.

Tony Curtis

Hollywood obits are regularly in the high 80s – these are people who live a long time, which is what happens if you don't smoke, you work out every day, you get your body fat awesomely low and you do only the best cocaine.

David Thomson

Golden Oldies

FAMOUS OLDIES

I have enjoyed greatly the second blooming that comes when you finish the life of the emotions and of personal relations, and suddenly find – at the age of 50, say – that a whole new life has opened before you, filled with things you can think about, study, or read about … It is as if a fresh sap of ideas and thoughts was rising in you.

Agatha Christie

When you're a young man, Macbeth is a character part. When you're older, it's a straight part.

Laurence Olivier

Old age is like everything else. To make a success of it, you've got to start young.

Fred Astaire

Golden Oldies

I have the body of an 18-year-old. I keep it in the fridge.

Spike Milligan

One of the advantages of ageing is losing obsession about work and being able to spend some more time with your family.

Clint Eastwood

In his later years Pablo Picasso was not allowed to roam an art gallery unattended, for he had previously been discovered in the act of trying to improve on one of his old masterpieces.

Anon

You can't be as old as I am without waking up with a surprised look on your face every morning: 'Holy Christ, what da ya know – I'm still around!' It's absolutely amazing that I survived all the booze and smoking and the cars and the career.

Paul Newman

I used to desire many, many things, but now I have just one desire, and that's to get rid of all my other desires.

John Cleese

I shall not waste my days in trying to prolong them.

Ian L. Fleming

These days I am a teetotal, mean-spirited, right-wing, narrow-minded, conservative Christian bigot, but not a racist.

Jane Russell, speaking in 2003

I look forward to being older, when what you look like becomes less and less an issue and what you are is the point.

Susan Sarandon

Hollywood will accept actresses playing 10 years older, but actors can play 10 years younger.

Greta Scacchi

I have no regrets. I wouldn't have lived my life the way I did if I was going to worry about what people were going to say.

Ingrid Bergman

At my age I do what Mark Twain did. I get my daily paper, look at the obituaries page and if I'm not there I carry on as usual.

Patrick Moore

Golden Oldies

I feel like an old geezer! Well, I am an old geezer.

Terry Wogan

I am affectionately known by Elton John as either Sylvia Disc or the Bionic Christian.

Sir Cliff Richard

In two years time I will be 50. But age doesn't hold any terrors for me because I feel stronger than ever.

Pierce Brosnan

I am not young enough to know everything.

Oscar Wilde

I will never give in to old age until I become old. And I'm not old yet!

Tina Turner

Getting old is a fascination thing. The older you get, the older you want to get.

Keith Richards

With 60 staring me in the face, I have developed inflammation of the sentence structure and a definite hardening of the paragraphs.

James Thurber

I love life because what more is there.

Anthony Hopkins

I am not the first man who wanted to make changes in his life at 60 and I won't be the last. It is just that others can do it with anonymity.

Harrison Ford

Everyone says I'm terrified of getting old but the truth is that in my job becoming old and extinct are one and the same thing.

Cher

My mother, God rest her soul, as soon as you gave her something, she would be eyeing it up to see who she could give it to when they turned up and she didn't have a present for them. You could see the virtual wrapping paper going around the thing you bought... you could see it was on its way to Doris next door.

Maureen Lipman, Grumpy Old Women

No sophisticated time schedule any more, that is something marvellous. Just cooking noodles, cultivating tomatoes, playing golf, lying in bed, eating chips with ketchup and spooning up peanut butter directly from the glass.

Celine Dion

Golden Oldies

I will actually say, 'Look, I'm very old and I'm very bored with you all, and I'm leaving.' It's one of the advantages of ageing – you can be eccentric and rude.

Sheila Hancock, Grumpy Old Women

Wouldn't it be great if people could get to live suddenly as often as they die suddenly?

Katharine Hepburn

Professionally, I have no age.

Kathleen Turner

I think I'm finally growing up – and about time.

Elizabeth Taylor

It is far better to be out with beautiful girls than be an old fart in the pub talking about what you were like in the 60s.

Mick Jagger

There are very little things in this life I cannot afford and patience is one of them.

Larry Hagman

Because young men are so goddamn disappointing!

Harrison Ford, explaining why women like older leading men

Things hurt me now. My knees hurt, my back hurts. But your head still thinks it's 23.

George Clooney

Harrison Ford may be getting old, but he can fight like a 28-year-old man.

Harrison Ford

Music

The Rolling Stones are on tour again. They were gonna call the tour 'The Rolling Stones Live Plus Keith Richards'.

David Letterman

—What do you think John Lennon would have been like at 64?
—He would be just John – all that he was before. But I think talking about a person's age is ageism, like racism or sexism. It isolates attitudes.

Yoko Ono

The Rolling Stones are on tour again. They were gonna call the tour 'Hey! You! Get Offa My Stairlift!'

David Letterman

Music

I'm always asked, 'What about being too old to rock 'n' roll?' Presumably lots of writers get better as they get older. So why shouldn't I?

Lou Reed

The Rolling Stones are on tour again. They were gonna call the tour 'And You Thought Aerosmith Was Old'.

David Letterman

I can still rock like a son of a bitch.

Ozzy Osbourne

The Rolling Stones are on tour again. They were gonna call the tour 'We Live Through the Concert or Your Money Back'.

David Letterman

The Grateful Dead are like bad architecture or an old whore. Stick around long enough and you eventually get respectable.

Jerry Garcia

The Rolling Stones are on tour again. They were gonna call the tour 'Brown Sugar and Lots of Bran'.

David Letterman

When I give concerts, I ask women not to throw their knickers at me. At my age, I don't want to be a caricature of myself.

Tom Jones

The Rolling Stones are on tour again. They were gonna call the tour 'Under-45s Not Admitted Without a Parent'.

David Letterman

People are always talking about when the Rolling Stones should retire, but it's a racial thing. Nobody ever says B.B. King is too old to play. It's like you can't be white and be an old rock 'n' roller.

David Bailey

The Rolling Stones are on tour again. They were gonna call the tour 'Come Half-Price if You're Mick Jagger's Illegitimate Child'.

David Letterman

Times have changed. Nowadays, when people talk about the stones I want to know if they mean gall or kidney.

Cliff Renwick

The Rolling Stones are on tour again. They were gonna call the tour 'The $140 Million in the Bank Isn't Enough'.

David Letterman

Holding Back the Years

Old Father Time will turn you into a hag if you don't show the bitch who's boss.

Mae West

I don't plan to grow old gracefully. I plan to have face-lifts until my ears meet.

Rita Rudner

I see a lot of new faces. Especially on the old faces.

Johnny Carson

In Los Angeles, people don't get older, they just get tighter.

Greg Proops

I've had so much plastic surgery, if I have one more face-lift it will be a caesarean.

Phyllis Diller

I wish I had a twin, so I could know what I'd look like without plastic surgery.

Joan Rivers

Now I'm getting older I take health supplements: geranium, dandelion, passionflower, hibiscus. I feel great, and when I pee, I experience the fresh scent of potpourri.

Sheila Wenz

—I gave Maris botox injections as a gift for our wedding anniversary one year.
—Oh, yes, probably your 10th. That's 'Toxins', isn't it?

Niles and Frasier Crane, Frasier

Moisturisers do work. The rest is pap. There is nothing on God's earth that will take away 30 years of arguing with your husband.

Anita Roddick

Wrinkle cream doesn't work. I've been using it for two years and my balls still look like raisins.

Harland Williams

Anti-wrinkle cream there may be, but anti-fat-bastard cream there is not.

Dave, The Full Monty

The best anti-ageing cream is ice cream. What other food makes you feel like you're 8 years old again?

Anon

Holding Back the Years

The easiest way to diminish the appearance of wrinkles is to keep your glasses off when you look in the mirror.

Joan Rivers

A woman I graduated from college with told me plastic surgery was vulgar, that lines were a sign of character, that it's beautiful to age. I said bull. Character is internal. If you want to present yourself to the world with a face-lift, why the hell not?

Judith Krantz

Everyone in Tinseltown is getting pinched, lifted and pulled. The trade-off is that something of your soul in your face goes away. You end up looking body-snatched.

Robert Redford

I call them the lizard women. They're the ones who have had so much cosmetic surgery that they're no longer biodegradable. They look like giant Komodo dragons with Chanel accessories.

Brett Butler

I wish it were okay in this country to look one's age, whatever it is. Maturity has a lot going for it. For example, you no longer get bubblegum stuck in your brace.

Cyra McFadden

I've not had any surgery. I am too curious to find out exactly how I progress every day of my life naturally. As I've always said, don't fuck around with God.

Elaine Stritch

I love my wife's wrinkles because I know where they come from. Wrinkles are the medals you've won in the battle that is life.

John Peel

How foolish to think that one can ever slam the door in the face of age. Much wiser to be polite and gracious and ask him to lunch in advance.

Noël Coward

To keep the heart unwrinkled, to be hopeful, kindly, cheerful, reverent – that is to triumph over old age.

Thomas Bailey Aldrich

Young at Heart

He says he feels young at heart but slightly older in other places.

Anon

Young at Heart

Another belief of mine: that everyone else my age is an adult, whereas I am merely in disguise.

Margaret Atwood

You can't help getting older, but you don't have to get old.

George Burns

You're only young once, but you can be immature forever.

John Greier

One starts to get young at the age of 60 and then it is too late.

Pablo Picasso

When I was 10, I read fairy tales in secret and would have been ashamed if I had been found doing so. Now that I am 50, I read them openly. When I became a man, I put away childish things – including the fear of childishness and the desire to be grown-up.

C. S. Lewis

Setting a good example for your children takes all the fun out of middle age.

William Feather

I have spent my whole life – up to a minute ago – being younger than I am now.

John Ciardi

Except for an occasional heart attack I feel as young as I ever did.

Robert Benchley

Try to keep your soul young and quivering right up to old age.

George Sand

Life would be infinitely happier if we could only be born at the age of 80 and gradually approach 18.

Mark Twain

The Fountain of Youth

My recipe for perpetual youth? I've never had my face in the sun, and I have a very handsome young husband … Sex is one of the best and cheapest beauty treatments there is.

Joan Collins

The Fountain of Youth

The secret of my youthful appearance is simply – mashed swede. As a face-mask, as a nightcap, and in an emergency, as a draught-excluder.

Kitty, Victoria Wood

Jewellery takes people's minds off your wrinkles.

Sonja Henie

Jewellery should be bold. Neat little pearls can add 10 years.

Joan Collins

If you don't want to get old, don't mellow.

Linda Ellerbee

To have the respect of my peers and the admiration of young people beats plastic surgery any day.

Johnny Cash

The fountain of youth is a mixture of gin and vermouth.

Cole Porter

With them I'm Jack Nicholson. Without them I'm fat and 60.

Jack Nicholson on his trademark sunglasses

You're only as young as the last time you changed your mind.

Timothy Leary

It's very ageing to talk about age.

Merle Oberon

There is a fountain of youth: it is your mind, your talents, the creativity you bring to your life and the lives of the people you love. When you learn to tap this source, you will truly have defeated age.

Sophia Loren

An inordinate passion for pleasure is the secret of remaining young.

Oscar Wilde

People are living longer because of the decline in religion. Not many people believe in the hereafter, so they keep going.

Cyril Clarke

One of the secrets of a long and fruitful life is to forgive everybody everything every night before you go to bed.

Bernard M. Baruch

The Fountain of Youth

I have only managed to live so long by carrying no hatreds.

Winston Churchill

Old people who shine from inside look 10 to 20 years younger.

Dolly Parton

As long as you can still be disappointed, you are still young.

Sarah Churchill

Whatever a man's age, he can reduce it several years by putting a bright-coloured flower in his buttonhole.

Mark Twain

At my age flowers scare me.

George Burns

If you want to stay young-looking, pick your parents very carefully.

Dick Clark

The secret of salvation in old age is this: keep sweet, keep useful, and keep busy.

Elbert Hubbard

The secret to old age: you have to know what you're going to do the next day.

Louis J. Lefkowitz

You are young at any age if you are planning for tomorrow. I take inspiration from that wonderful Scottish actor Finlay Currie. Shortly before he died at the age of 90, he was asked on a TV chat show if he'd ever played a romantic lead. 'Not yet, laddie,' he replied. 'Not yet.'

Bob Monkhouse

Humour keeps the elderly rolling along, singing a song. When you laugh, it's an involuntary explosion of the lungs. The lungs need to replenish themselves with oxygen. So you laugh, you breathe, the blood runs, and everything is circulating. If you don't laugh, you'll die.

Mel Brooks

I love to laugh. I think laughter can cure. Either the lines go up or they go down. If they go up, that's a good sign.

Elizabeth Taylor

The heart is the real Fountain of Youth.

Mark Twain

The Fountain of Youth

The secret of staying young is to live honestly, eat slowly, and lie about your age.

Lucille Ball

I don't think the trick is staying young. I think the trick is ageing well.

Dr Thomas Perls

We must establish the idea that it is important to look well, not to look young. It is no more a compliment to say you don't look your age than to say you don't look Jewish or you don't look like an American.

Karen Decrow

—Must you leave so early?
—I must, if I am to keep my youth.
—But why didn't you bring him with you? I should be delighted to meet him.

Lady Cunard and Somerset Maugham

I believe in loyalty. When a woman reaches a certain age she likes, she should stick with it.

Eva Gabor

The trick is growing up without growing old.

Casey Stengel

I was wise enough to never grow up while fooling most people into believing I had.

Margaret Mead

The best thing about growing older is that it takes such a long time.

Anon

She was a handsome woman of 45 and would remain so for many years.

Anita Brookner

By the time I'd grown up, I naturally supposed that I'd grown up.

Eve Babitz

Being loved keeps you young.

Madonna

I'm saving that rocker for the day when I feel as old as I really am.

Dwight D. Eisenhower

I'm not denying my age, I'm embellishing my youth.

Tamara Reynolds

Maturity

In an ideal world I would like to be alive until I am dead.

Sir John Harvey-Jones

Cheerfulness and contentment are great beautifiers, and are famous preservers of youthful looks.

Charles Dickens

Pushing 40? She's hanging on for dear life.

Ivy Compton-Burnett

She has discovered the secret of perpetual middle age.

Oscar Levant

Maturity

You grow up the day you have the first real laugh – at yourself.

Ethel Barrymore

The first sign of maturity is the discovery that the volume knob also turns to the left.

Jerry Wright

Maturity

You know you've grown up when you become obsessed with the thermostat.

Jeff Foxworthy

What I look forward to is continued immaturity followed by death.

Dave Barry

Age is a very high price to pay for maturity.

Tom Stoppard

Tony Benn immatures with age.

Harold Wilson

No one is ever old enough to know better.

Holbrook Jackson

When I grow up I want to be a little boy.

Joseph Heller

A person's maturity consists in having found again the seriousness one had as a child at play.

Friedrich Wilhelm Nietzsche

Over the Hill

I'm so old they've cancelled my blood type.

Bob Hope

I'd rather be over the hill than under it.

Anon

To live beyond 80 is an exaggeration, almost an excess.

Antonio Callado

Wrecked on the lee shore of age.

Sarah Orne Jewett

Just remember, once you're over the hill you begin to pick up speed.

Charles M. Schulz

You know you're over the hill when the only whistles you get are from the tea kettle.

Anon

The follies which a man regrets most in his life are those which he didn't commit when he had the opportunity.

Helen Rowland

I didn't get old on purpose, it just happened. If you're lucky it could happen to you.

Andy Rooney

A lot of people start to fall to bits at 30 … quite honestly, once you are able to reproduce you're over the hill. You start to go downhill at 18 physically.

Mick Jagger

Over the hill? I don't remember any hill?!

Anon

I'm too beat-up and old now to be a sex symbol.

Mel Gibson

I've been around so long I can remember Doris Day before she was a virgin.

Groucho Marx

I'm too old for this sh*t!

Danny Glover, as Roger Murtaugh, Lethal Weapon

You're not over the hill until you hear your favourite songs in an elevator.

Anon

My veins are filled once a week with a Neapolitan carpet cleaner distilled from the Adriatic and I am as bald as an egg. However, I still get around and am mean to cats.

John Cheever

Listen to Your Elders

Look to the future, because that is where you'll spend the rest of your life.

George Burns

Don't take life too seriously; you'll never get out of it alive.

Elbert Hubbard

You can add years to your life by wearing your pants backwards.

Johnny Carson

Don't smoke too much, drink too much, eat too much or work too much. We're all on the road to the grave – but there's no need to be in the passing lane.

Robert Orben

Stay humble. Always answer your phone – no matter who else is in the car.

Jack Lemmon

Listen to Your Elders

My mum died about three years ago at the age of 101, and just towards the end, as she began to run out of energy, she did actually stop trying to tell me what to do most of the time.

John Cleese

Forget past mistakes. Forget failures. Forget everything except what you are going to do now and do it.

William Durant

Do not do unto others as you expect they should do unto you; their tastes may not be the same.

George Bernard Shaw

First law on holes – when you're in one, stop digging.

Denis Healey

If at first you don't succeed, try, try again. Then quit. No use being a damn fool about it.

W. C. Fields

How people keep correcting us when we are young! There is always some bad habit or other they tell us we ought to get over. Yet most bad habits are tools to help us through life.

Jack Nicklaus

Listen to Your Elders

It is better to die on your feet than to live on your knees.

Dolores Ibarruri

The time to begin most things is 10 years ago.

Mignon McLaughlin

Never think you've seen the last of anything.

Eudora Welty

There are times not to flirt. When you're sick. When you're with children. When you're on the witness stand.

Joyce Jillson

Be bold. If you're going to make an error, make a doozey, and don't be afraid to hit the ball.

Billie Jean King

Find an aim in life before you run out of ammunition.

Arnold Glasow

I don't know the key to success, but the key to failure is trying to please everybody.

Bill Cosby

Always read stuff that will make you look good if you die in the middle of it.

P.J. O'Rourke

Never kick a fresh turd on a hot day.

Harry S. Truman

Be careful about reading health books. You might die of a misprint.

Mark Twain

Take the goods the gods provide, and don't stand and sulk when they are snatched away.

Mary McMullen

Go through your phone book, call people and ask them to drive you to the airport. The ones who will drive you are your true friends. The rest aren't bad people; they're just acquaintances.

Jay Leno

Be equal to your talent, not your age. At times let the gap between them be embarrassing.

Yevgeny Yevtushenko

At 46 one must be a miser; only have time for essentials.

Virginia Woolf

You can't have everything. Where would you put it?

Steven Wright

Listen to Your Elders

In real life, I assure you, there is no such thing as algebra.

Fran Lebowitz

Sometimes the road less travelled is less travelled for a reason.

Jerry Seinfeld

Never pick a fight with an ugly person. They've got nothing to lose.

Robin Williams

You can observe a lot just by watching.

Yogi Berra

There are only two ways of telling the complete truth – anonymously and posthumously.

Thomas Sowell

When you get to the end of your rope, tie a knot and hang on.

Franklin D. Roosevelt

Don't worry about the world coming to an end today. It's already tomorrow in Australia.

Charles M. Schulz

Be who you are and say what you feel, because those who mind don't matter and those who matter don't mind.

Dr Seuss

You're only given a little spark of madness. You mustn't lose it.

Robin Williams

Son, always tell the truth. Then you'll never have to remember what you said the last time.

Sam Rayburn

Whatever you want to do, do it now. There are only so many tomorrows.

Michael Landon

Act Your Age

The older you get, the more important it is not to act your age.

Ashleigh Brilliant

We don't stop playing because we grow old, we grow old because we stop playing.

George Bernard Shaw

Act Your Age

I've always believed the secret of eternal youth is arrested development.

Alice Roosevelt Longworth

The ageing process has you firmly in its grasp if you never get the urge to throw a snowball.

Doug Larson

Even though I'm very old, I always feel like the youngest person in the room.

W. H. Auden

To be young, really young, takes a very long time.

Pablo Picasso

The secret of genius is to carry the spirit of the child into old age, which means never losing your enthusiasm.

Aldous Huxley

The great man is one who never loses his child's heart.

Mencius

I have the heart of a small child. I keep it in a jar on my desk.

Stephen King

You Can Teach an Old Dog New Tricks

When I was young I was amazed at Plutarch's statement that the elder Cato began at the age of 80 to learn Greek. I am amazed no longer. Old age is ready to undertake tasks that youth shirked because they would take too long.

W. Somerset Maugham

I enjoy going to the centre because I always get a lovely smile from the ladies there and I can impress them with new computer tips.

Lady, 100, attending computer classes

You are never too old. One of many examples, Grandma Moses (1860–1961), she started painting in her late 70s. She is best known for her documentary paintings of rural life. If you ever think you are too old, think of Grandma Moses!

Catherine Pulsifer

You are never too old to set another goal or to dream a new dream.

Les Brown

I'm having difficulty getting the doctors around here to sign the appropriate form.

Spike Milligan, on seeking permission to celebrate his 80th birthday with a 12,000 foot skydive.

I'm Not Menthyl

MALAPROPISMS

My nan, God bless 'er, gets things a bit mixed up. She said to me the other day, 'I've bought one of those new George Formby grills.'

Peter Kay

—Barbara, didn't Elsie next door have implants?
—No, eggplants, Mam.

Nana and Barbara Royle, The Royle Family

My mother thinks a crouton's a Japanese sofa.

Mary Unfaithful

—He's autistic, Gran.
—That's nice. I wish I could draw.

Martin and Millicent Smith

Our Susan's still not had her baby. If she doesn't have it soon she'll have to be seduced.

Brenda Sneddon

Mark my words: her chickens will come home to roast.

Coral Greene

My mum said, 'I saw whatsaname last week, oh, whatshisname, I can never remember anything these days – it's this damned anorexia.'

Stephen Fry

I can't be doin' with Donny Osmond and that bunch of Morons.

Bert Fletcher

My nan was complaining of chest pains. I said, 'Are you all right, Nan?' She said, 'I think I've got vagina.'

Peter Kay

Oh, love, can you get me some of that cunnilinctus for my cough?

Edna Steele

I've got bigger fish to fly!

Elsie Mason

I'm Not Menthyl

The patio doors are sticking again. Have you got some of that UB40?

Phyllis Amison

The doctor says I have to have a hearing aid because there's a blockage in my Euston station tube.

Joe Hadley

I don't want to see a pieciatrist; I'm not menthyl!

Hylda Baker, Nearest and Dearest

I don't want to end up in an old folk's home wearing incompetence pads. I'm still compost mentis.

Harriet Wynn

An elderly lady came into the chemist and asked for a bottle of euthanasia. I didn't say anything. I just handed her a bottle of echinacea.

Lydia Berryman

SENIOR MOMENTS

For those of you haven't read the book, it's being published tomorrow.

David Frost

And there's the Victoria Memorial, built as a memorial to Victoria.

David Dimbleby

Richard Burton had a tremendous passion for the English language, especially the spoken and written word.

Frank Bough

It will take time to restore chaos and order.

George W. Bush

Beginning in February 1976 your assistance benefits will be discontinued ... Reason: it has been reported to our office that you expired on January 1, 1976.

Excerpt from a letter, Illinois Department of Public Aid

My shoes are size two and a half, the same size as my feet.

Elaine Page

I didn't know *Onward Christian Soldiers* was a Christian song.

Aggie Pate, at a non-denominational mayor's breakfast, Fort Worth, Texas

I'm Not Menthyl

The Holocaust was an obscene period in our nation's history … this century's history … We all lived in this century. I didn't live in this century.

Dan Quayle

Was it you or your brother who was killed in the war?

Rev. William Spooner

Fiction writing is great. You can make up almost anything.

Ivana Trump, upon finishing her first novel

A bachelor's life is no life for a single man.

Samuel Goldwyn

I love California; I practically grew up in Phoenix.

Dan Quayle

You seem to be a man who likes to keep his feet on the ground – you sail a lot.

Alan Titchmarsh

The Rolling Stones suffered a great loss with the death of Ian Stewart, the man who had for so many years played piano quietly and silently with them on stage.

Andy Peebles

Elderly American lady: 'You speak very good English.'
Me: 'Thank you, but that's because I come from the United Kingdom.'
Elderly American lady: 'Oh, I didn't know they teach English over there.'

Anon

Republicans understand the importance of bondage between a mother and child.

Dan Quayle

Cardial – as in cardial arrest.

Eve Pollard

Your ambition – is that right – is to abseil across the English Channel?

Cilla Black

I haven't read any of the autobiographies about me.

Elizabeth Taylor

The nice thing about being senile is you can hide your own Easter eggs.

Anon

To see what is in front of one's nose needs a constant struggle.

George Orwell

I'm Not Menthyl

I never know how much of what I say is true.

Bette Midler

The future ain't what it used to be.

Yogi Berra

I am wonderful, with a perfect physique, very charming, rich and look like Jude Law.

Peter Stringfellow

I've always thought that underpopulated countries in Africa are vastly underpolluted.

Lawrence Summers, chief economist of the World Bank

He hits from both sides of the plate. He's amphibious.

Yogi Berra

One year ago today, the time for excuse-making has come to an end.

George W. Bush

It's always been my dream to come to Madison Square Garden and be the warm-up act for Elvis.

Al Gore

Outside of the killings, Washington has one of the lowest crime rates in the country.

Mayor Marion Barry, Washington, D.C.

I haven't committed a crime. What I did was fail to comply with the law.

David Dinkins, New York City Mayor

And so, in my State of the – my State of the Union – or state – my speech to the nation, whatever you want to call it, speech to the nation – I asked Americans to give 4,000 years – 4,000 hours over the next – the rest of your life – of service to America. That's what I asked – 4,000 hours.

George W. Bush

Abortion is advocated only by persons who have themselves been born.

Ronald Reagan

Money

When I was young, I thought money was the most important thing in life. Now that I'm old, I know it is.

Oscar Wilde

Don't grow old without money, honey.

Lena Horne

Money

If you're given the choice between money and sex appeal, take the money. As you get older, the money will become your sex appeal.

Katharine Hepburn

Three things have helped me successfully through the ordeals of life: an understanding husband, a good analyst, and millions of dollars.

Mary Tyler Moore

If you think nobody cares whether you are alive or dead, try missing a couple of car payments.

Ann Landers

I have enough money to last me the rest of my life – unless I have to buy something.

Jackie Mason

There are no luggage-racks on hearses, no pockets in shrouds.

Anon

Money isn't everything, but it sure keeps you in touch with your children.

J. Paul Getty

I've got all the money I'll ever need if I die by four o'clock this afternoon.

Henny Youngman

Money is something you have to make in case you don't die.

Max Asnas

I'm living so far beyond my income that we may almost be said to be living apart.

e.e. cummings

There's no reason to be the richest man in the cemetery. You can't do any business from there.

Colonel Sanders

Another good thing about being poor is that when you are 70 your children will not have declared you legally insane in order to gain control of your estate.

Woody Allen

Most men love money and security more, and creation and construction less, as they get older.

John Maynard Keynes

Parents should be given only a modest and sensible allowance. And they should be encouraged to save up for things. This builds character. It also helps pay for the funeral.

P.J. O'Rourke

Women on Ageing

I have to be careful to get out before I become the grotesque caricature of a hatchet-faced woman with big knockers.

Jamie Lee Curtis

I shall not grow conservative with age.

Elizabeth Cady Stanton

No one can avoid ageing, but ageing productively is something else.

Katherine Graham

A woman my age is not supposed to be attractive or sexually appealing. I just get kinda tired of that.

Kathleen Turner

At last now you can be what the old cannot recall and the young long for in dreams, yet still include them all.

Elizabeth Jennings

When I passed 40 I dropped pretence, 'cause men like women who got some sense.

Maya Angelou

A woman's always younger than a man at equal years.

Elizabeth Barrett Browning

Old age, believe me, is a good and pleasant thing. It is true you are gently shouldered off the stage, but then you are given such a comfortable front stall as spectator.

Jane Harrison

You couldn't live 82 years in the world without being disillusioned.

Rebecca West, at age 82

I do resent that when you're in the most cool, powerful time of your life, which is your 40s, you're put out to pasture. I think women are so much cooler when they're older. So it's a drag that we're not allowed to age.

Rosanna Arquette

I am really looking forward as I get older and older, to being less and less nice.

Annette Bening

Women on Ageing

When you're young, you just go right along. When you're older, you think, they've switched the rules on me.

Linda Evans

You know, when I first went into the movies Lionel Barrymore played my grandfather. Later he played my father and finally he played my husband. If he had lived I'm sure I would have played his mother. That's the way it is in Hollywood. The men get younger and the women get older.

Lillian Gish

The older I get, the more of my mother I see in myself.

Nancy Friday

You take your life in your own hands, and what happens? A terrible thing: no one to blame.

Erica Jong

I spend most of my time puffing up my ego … till I'm this big ego thing … but it doesn't take much for it to be pricked, and then I'm just this deflated, shrivelled, shamed old woman with a bit of wee running down my legs.

Jenny Eclair, Grumpy Old Women

I have become more vocal in my complaining. I now say, 'This is not working for me.' This is my new sentence ... It's just letting them know it's all about you, and for you, it's not working.

India Knight, Grumpy Old Women

I do write a hell of a lot of letters of complaint. I haven't really got time to do it, but I find it gets rid of some of my rage.

Sheila Hancock, Grumpy Old Women

Life is more interesting. When you're self-involved and you see yourself centre-stage all the time, you're in agonies of self-consciousness, you're really concerned: how do I look? How do I sound? It's wonderful not to care about that any more.

Germaine Greer

You end up as you deserve. In old age you must put up with the face, the friends, the health, and the children you have earned.

Fay Weldon

Do not deprive me of my age. I have earned it.

May Sarton

Women on Ageing

Being 70 is not a sin.

Golda Meir

One of the many things nobody ever tells you about middle age is that it's such a nice change from being young.

Dorothy Canfield Fisher

It is not all bad, this getting old, ripening. After the fruit has got its growth it should juice up and mellow. God forbid I should live long enough to ferment and rot and fall to the ground in a squash.

Emily Carr

As a lady of a certain age, I am willing to let the photographers and their zoom lenses stay, but only if they use their Joan Collins lens on me for close-ups.

Kay Ullrich

Every woman over 50 should stay in bed until noon.

Mamie Eisenhower

I've had to tone it down a bit. But I've still got fabulous legs and wear mini-skirts. I'll keep wearing bikinis till I'm 80 … I will grow old gracefully in public – and disgracefully in private.

Jerry Hall

Men on Ageing

I don't want to be the oldest performer in captivity ... I don't want to look like a little old man dancing out there.

Fred Astaire

When our memories outweigh our dreams, we have grown old.

Bill Clinton

That sign of old age, extolling the past at the expense of the present.

Sydney Smith

Men become old, but they never become good.

Oscar Wilde

As men get older, their toys get more expensive.

Marvin Davis

You get older and suddenly you don't have to go out and do all that sh*t you do when you're young and dumb. Because now you're old and dumb instead.

Johnny Depp

Men on Ageing

Old age, calm, expanded, broad with the haughty breadth of the universe, old age flowing free with the delicious nearby freedom of death.

Walt Whitman

When they came with the collection plate, they walked right past me like I was a penniless mugger.

Jimmy Savile, on attending Christmas Mass

The older we grow, the greater become the ordeals.

Johann Wolfgang von Goethe

A man over 90 is a great comfort to all his elderly neighbours: he is a picket-guard at the extreme outpost; and the young folks of 60 and 70 feel that the enemy must get by him before he can come near their camp.

Oliver Wendell Holmes

I've been grumpy since the age of 10, so it wasn't a generational shift. I never expect anything to get better. I just am grumpy.

Sir Bob Geldof

I didn't turn into, at the age of 30, a grumpy old man. I was a grumpy teenager as well.

Rory McGrath

Every man desires to live long; but no man would be old.

Jonathan Swift

I think a lot about getting old. I don't want to be one of those 70-year-olds who still want lots of sex.

Rupert Everett

If we spent as much time feeling positive about getting older as we do trying to stay young, how much different our lives would be.

Rob Brown

I think when the full horror of being 50 hits you, you should stay home and have a good cry.

Alan Bleasdale

Perhaps being old is having lighted rooms inside your head, and people in them, acting. People you know yet can't quite name.

Philip Larkin

I have found it to be true that the older I've become the better my life has become.

Rush Limbaugh

Men on Ageing

I think in 20 years I'll be looked at like Bob Hope. Doing those president jokes and golf sh*t. It scares me.

Eddie Murphy

At my age, I want to wake up and see sunshine pouring in through the windows every day.

John Cleese

Age is not a particularly interesting subject. Anyone can get old. All you have to do is live long enough.

Groucho Marx

Some mornings, it's just not worth chewing through the leather straps.

Emo Philips

As I get older I seem to believe less and less and yet to believe what I do believe more and more.

Gerald Brenan

You feel a little older in the morning. By noon I feel about 55.

Bob Dole

I still find each day too short for all the thoughts I want to think, all the walks I want to take, all the books I want to read, and all the friends I want to see.

John Burroughs

The more defects a man may have, the older he is, the less lovable, the more resounding his success.

Marquis de Sade

Few people know how to be old.

François de La Rochefoucauld

Most men do not mature, they simply grow taller.

Leo Rosten

I am my age. I'm not making any effort to change it.

Harrison Ford

The older I get, the more I become an apple-pie, sparkling-cider kind of guy.

Scott Foley

A man can be much amused when he hears himself seriously called an old man for the first time.

T. Kinnes

Men on Ageing

Age is how you feel. If you take care of yourself, you'll be able to do the same things. You may not do it as often. But you can still do it.

Barry Bonds

Nobody went out to pasture, and a lot of people are doing their best work. Bruce Springsteen, Tom Petty and Sting are at the top of their game. I mean, Tony Bennett is the coolest guy I ever met! We have to figure out how to break out of this age ghetto.

Bonnie Raitt

I know I can't cheat death, but I can cheat old age.

Darwin Deason

I like men who have a future and women who have a past.

Oscar Wilde

As one grows older, one must try not to work oneself to death unnecessarily. At least that's how it is with me … I can scarcely keep pace and must watch out that the creative forces do not chase me around the universe in a wallop.

Carl Jung

Men on Ageing

Men of my age live in a state of continual desperation.

Trevor McDonald

Old age is an insult. It's like being smacked.

Lawrence Durrell

Old age: I fall asleep during the funerals of my friends.

Mason Cooley

I don't think I've gotten any smarter, but your reflexes slow down before you do something stupid when you're older.

Kris Kristofferson

I'm only two years older than Brad Pitt, but I look a lot older, which used to greatly frustrate me. It doesn't any more.

George Clooney

They're of a certain age, these ladies. You know, past their procreational best.

Ian McCaskill, discussing his admirers

Old age scares me. Almost everyone I know who is old is quite miserable, especially men.

Rupert Everett

Pleasures and Perks of Growing Older

As you grow old, you lose interest in sex, your friends drift away, and your children often ignore you. There are other advantages, of course, but these are the outstanding ones.

Richard Needham

—You know the best thing about being old?
—Cardigans?
—No. Disabled parking spaces.

Anon

One compensation of old age is that it excuses you from picnics.

William Feather

One of the delights of being a senior citizen is it's easy to annoy young people. Step 1: get in the car. Step 2: turn the indicator on. Step 3: leave it on for 50 miles.

David Letterman

I can't wait to get old enough to ride in one of those buggies at the airport. Whizzing past all those poor sods on the long trek to the departure gate. It will make being old worthwhile.

Sean Needham

One good thing about being old and having a failing memory is that I can enjoy the endless repeats of programmes like *Inspector Morse*, *Murder She Wrote*, and *Midsomer Murders* because I can never remember whodunit.

Larry Simpkins

One of the good things about getting older is that you find you're more interesting than most of the people you meet.

Lee Marvin

I basically enjoy getting older because I get smarter. So what I have to say is more worth listening to, in my opinion.

Clive James

I used to dread getting older because I thought I would not be able to do all the things I wanted to do, but now that I am older I find that I don't want to do them.

Nancy Astor, 80

Pleasures and Perks of Growing Older

One of the delights known to age, and beyond the grasp of youth, is that of Not Going.

J. B. Priestley

By the bye, as I must leave off being young, I find many Douceurs in being a sort of Chaperon for I am put on the Sofa near the fire & can drink as much wine as I like.

Jane Austen

My husband's idea of a good night out is a good night in.

Maureen Lipman

I think happiness is easier to come by when you're older. Go for a nice walk and do some push-ups. Sex is always good. A hamburger will work, if you make it right and make it yourself. It should be rare and have raw onion and a lot of mustard. A martini, just one, is really fabulous. Going to Mass on Sunday morning, if it is the right sort of Mass, when the homily is short and the choir hangs together just right … Sleep. Sleep is always good. You almost always feel better when you wake up. Baseball games. And Louis Armstrong…

Garrison Keillor

One of the many pleasures of old age is giving things up.

Malcolm Muggeridge

I always make a point of starting the day at 6am with Champagne. It goes straight to the heart and cheers one up. White wine won't do. You need the bubbles.

John Mortimer

Pottering is the most fun you can have in slippers.

Guy Browning

I am getting to an age when I can only enjoy the last sport left. It is called hunting for your spectacles.

Lord Grey of Falloden

The great thing about being in your 70s is, what can they do to you? What have you got to lose? Freedom is just another word for having nothing left to lose.

Clint Eastwood

As a man grows older it is harder and harder to frighten him.

Jean Paul Richter

All one's life as a young woman one is on show, people notice you. You set yourself up to be noticed and admired. And then, not expecting it, you become middle aged and anonymous. No one notices you. You achieve a wonderful freedom. It is a positive thing. You can move about, unnoticed and invisible.

Doris Lessing

Pleasures and Perks of Growing Older

Bored? Here's a way the over-50 set can easily kill a good half hour: 1) Place your car keys in your right hand. 2) With your left hand call a friend and confirm a lunch or dinner date. 3) Hang up the phone. 4) Now look for your car keys.

Steve Martin

Now I'm getting older, I don't need to do drugs anymore. I can get the same effect just by standing up real fast.

Jonathan Katz

If I'm feeling really wild I don't bother flossing before bedtime.

Judith Viorst

My kitchen linoleum is so black and shiny that I waltz while I wait for the kettle to boil. This pleasure is for the old who live alone.

Florida Scott-Maxwell

A few perks of old age: things I buy now won't wear out; I enjoy hearing arguments about pensions; my secrets are safe with my friends because they can't remember them, either.

Felicity Muir

There's nothing like a flutter on the horses for a bit of excitement. Might raise the blood pressure but not as threatening as nicotine and alcohol.

Dorothy Norton

The nice thing about being old is that it doesn't affect your betting; in fact, old people betting makes more sense than young people betting. The lady in the bookie's said to me, 'Do you like having a little bet?' I told her no, I loathed it. I like to make big bets.

Clement Freud

One of my pleasures is to read in bed every night a few pages of P. G. Wodehouse, so that if I die in my sleep it will be with a smile on my face.

Arthur Marshall

One of the advantages of being 70 is that you need only four hours' sleep. True, you need it four times a day, but still.

Denis Norden

One good thing about getting older is that if you're getting married, the phrase 'till death do you part' doesn't sound so horrible. It only means about 10 or 15 years and not the eternity it used to mean.

Joy Behar

Pleasures and Perks of Growing Older

One of the greatest pleasures of growing old is looking back at the people you didn't marry.

Elizabeth Taylor

One of the pleasures of age is to find out that one was right, and that one was much righter than one knew at say 17 or 23.

Ezra Pound

The joy of being older is that in one's life one can, towards the end of the run, overact appallingly.

Quentin Crisp

Given three requisites – means of existence, reasonable health, and an absorbing interest – those years beyond 60 can be the happiest and most satisfying of a lifetime.

Earnest Calkins

Is not old wine wholesomest, old pippins toothsomest, old wood burns brightest, old linen wash whitest, and old lovers soundest?

John Webster

At 60 a man has passed most of the reefs and whirlpools. Excepting death, he has no enemies left to meet. That man has awakened to a new youth. He is young.

George Luks

Pleasures and Perks of Growing Older

We grow not older with years, but newer every day.

Emily Dickinson

The older you get, the better you get – unless you're a banana.

Anon

One positive thing about getting older is that you develop a sense of perspective about your legacy to future generations. People say things like, 'We're going to use up our Earth's resources. The Earth will be uninhabitable by 2050.' And I find myself nodding and going, 'No problem, I'll be dead.'

Dave Barry

As I move, graciously I hope, toward the door marked 'Exit', it occurs to me that the only thing I ever really liked to do was go to the movies.

Gore Vidal

Did you know that by the time he'd turned 80, Winston Churchill had coronary thrombosis, three attacks of pneumonia, a hernia, two strokes and something known as a senile itch? All the same, though often setting fire to himself, he still managed to enjoy a cigar.

Beryl Bainbridge

Pleasures and Perks of Growing Older

I smoke 10 to 15 cigars a day. At my age, if I don't have something to hang on to, I'll fall over.

George Burns

At the age of 80, there are very few pleasures left to me, but one of them is passive smoking.

Baroness Trumpington

But when I don't smoke I scarcely feel as if I'm living. I don't feel as if I'm living unless I'm killing myself.

Russell Hoban

I have every sympathy with the American who was so horrified by what he had read of the effects of smoking that he gave up reading.

Henry G. Strauss

I would reintroduce smoking everywhere.

Martin Burton, head of Zippo's Circus, tells Time Out *magazine how he would tackle being Mayor of London*

I don't smoke, but I'd rather be with my pals who do than sitting alone in a pub with no people and no atmosphere.

Brian Monteith, Conservative MSP for Mid-Scotland and Fife

At least by going to the jungle I won't have people telling me where and when I can smoke. Wish me luck and keep on smoking, if you want to.

Antony Worrall Thompson

My inspiration has always been Jeanne Calment, a Frenchwoman who smoked and drank every day and died a few years ago at the age of 122. When asked the secret of her longevity, she replied: 'I laugh a lot.' Well, you would, wouldn't you?

Victoria Coren

My doctor phoned and said you don't deserve this news, but your lungs are crystal-clear.

Chainsmoker Nicky Haslam, at age 63

Smokers of the world, unite! We have been bullied and nannied long enough. And if Tony Blair is tempted to follow the lead of Ireland and Italy, let us remind him that only 10.7 million voted Labour last time. But 15 million smoke.

Tom Utley

Smokers pay £19,000 a minute to the Exchequer, and that's enough to pay for the whole police force. Or to put it another way, for every £1 we cost the NHS, we give it £3.60. Please don't encourage the state to dictate how I live my life.

Jeremy Clarkson

I never allow myself to be photographed if I'm not smoking. It's a strict policy I've adhered to for a long time. I initiated it when it became politically correct not to smoke.

Maggi Hambling, on being photographed without a cigarette

I know Fabien [Barthez] smokes ... In England, it's a rare thing to see a player smoking but, all in all, I prefer that to an alcoholic.

Sir Alex Ferguson

When I smoked myself – up to 60 on some working days – I resolved never to become an anti-smoking bore because I hated them so much. By and large I've stuck to that: if people ask to smoke in our house we gladly cry, 'Yes, of course! Here are ashtrays, cigar clippers, pipe reamers, hookahs, oxygen masks – anything you need!'

Simon Hoggart

Apparently cigarettes contain embalming fluid. This explains why I'm possibly the best-preserved woman in Britain.

Sue Carroll

Smoking, I would now suggest, may be here to stay.

James Walton, editor of The Faber Book of Smoking

I used to smoke all the time, but four years ago I changed my smoking habit to smoke only when I'm drinking. However, this policy has had an adverse effect on my drinking habits.

Tommy Walsh

I might smoke more.

Jeremy Irons, announcing his New Year resolution

I enjoy it too much.

David Bowie, explaining why he will never give up smoking

If you want to smoke you should be allowed to do so. For those who smoke it is a natural, relaxing part of life.

Antony Worrall Thompson

When on occasion I'm asked by groups of aspiring writers what they should do to get on, my advice is always, emphatically, smoke. Smoke often and smoke with gusto. It's a little-known, indeed little-researched, fact of literature and journalism that no non-smoker is worth reading. And writers who give up become crashing bores.

A.A. Gill

Pleasures and Perks of Growing Older

Oh, I like smoking, I do. I smoke for my health, my mental health. Tobacco gives you little pauses, a rest from life. I don't suppose anyone smoking a pipe would have road rage, would they?

David Hockney

If I'm seen smoking in the street, people should come up to me and say thank you very much for keeping my tax bill down.

Jeremy Clarkson

I neither coughed nor felt sick. Instead, a sensation of well-being filled me, and I became slightly wired, not the reaction you get from alcohol, but sharper and calmer.

John Simpson, experiencing a cigar for the first time

Smoking is, if not my life, then at least my hobby. I love to smoke. Smoking is fun. Smoking is cool. Smoking is, as far as I'm concerned, the entire point of being an adult.

Fran Lebowitz

And a woman is only a woman, but a good cigar is a smoke.

Rudyard Kipling, The Betrothed

It is now proven, beyond a doubt, that smoking is a leading cause of statistics.

Fletcher Knebel

If I cannot smoke in heaven, then I shall not go.

Mark Twain

I want all hellions to quit puffing that hell fume in God's clean air.

Carry Nation

Having smoking and non-smoking sections in the same room is like having urinating and non-urinating sections in a swimming pool.

Ross Parker

I finally quit smoking by using the patch. I put six of them over my mouth.

Wendy Liebman

Giving up smoking is the easiest thing in the world. I know because I've done it thousands of times.

Mark Twain

They say if you smoke you knock off 10 years. But it's the last 10. What do you miss? The drooling years?

John Mendoza

Pleasures and Perks of Growing Older

I've been smoking for 30 years now and there's nothing wrong with my lung.

Freddie Starr

Smoking is very bad for you and should only be done because it looks so good. People who don't smoke have a terrible time finding something polite to do with their lips.

P.J. O'Rourke

—You're 86 years old. You smoke 10 cigars a day, drink five martinis a day, surround yourself with beautiful women. What does your doctor say about all this?
—My doctor is dead.

Interviewer and George Burns

If you resolve to give up smoking, drinking and loving, you don't actually live longer – it just seems longer.

Clement Freud

No pleasure is worth giving up for the sake of two more years in a geriatric home in Weston-super-Mare.

Kingsley Amis

The toll of time brings few delights in facing age's deadly spike; atop the list perhaps is this: outliving those we didn't like.

Art Buck

Pleasures and Perks of Growing Older

I feel very old sometimes. I carry on and would not like to die before having emptied a few more buckets of shit on the heads of my fellow men.

Gustave Flaubert

I advise you to go on living solely to enrage those who are paying your annuities. It is the only pleasure I have left. When I feel an attack of indigestion coming on, I picture two or three princes as gainers by my death, take courage out of spite, and conspire against them with rhubarb and temperance.

Voltaire

The older one grows, the more one likes indecency.

Virginia Woolf

I've got cheekier with age. You can get away with murder when you're 71 years old. People just think I'm a silly old fool.

Bernard Manning

At 50, the madwoman in the attic breaks loose, stomps down the stairs, and sets fire to the house. She won't be imprisoned anymore.

Erica Jong

Pleasures and Perks of Growing Older

Women may be the one group that grows more radical with age.

Gloria Steinem

I know I'm going to get old and be one of those crazy women who sits on balconies and spits on people and screams, 'Get a haircut!'

Carrie Fisher

Everything got better after I was 50. I wrote my best books. I walked Pillar, starting from Buttermere, which I'm told no fell-walker of advanced years should attempt.

A. J. P. Taylor

I sometimes think that God will ask us, 'That wonderful world of mine, why didn't you enjoy it more?'

Ronald Blythe

Good days are to be gathered like sunshine in grapes, to be trodden and bottled into wine and kept for age to sip at ease beside the fire. If the traveller has vintaged well, he need trouble to wander no longer; the ruby moments glow in his glass at will.

Freya Stark

Look at everything as though you were seeing it either for the first or last time. Then your time on earth will be filled with glory.

Betty Smith

Pleasures and Perks of Growing Older

The birds sing louder when you grow old.

Rose Chernin

When it is dark enough, you can see the stars.

Charles A. Beard

I am spending delightful afternoons in my garden, watching everything living around me. As I grow older, I feel everything departing, and I love everything with more passion.

Emile Zola

The happiness of finding idleness a duty. No more opinions, no more politics, no more practical tasks.

W. B. Yeats

Sometimes it's fun to sit in your garden and try to remember your dog's name.

Steve Martin

I've always thought that very few people grow old as admirably as academics. At least books never let them down.

Margaret Drabble

Pleasures and Perks of Growing Older

A truly great book should be read in youth, again in maturity and once more in old age, as a fine building should be seen by morning light, at noon and by moonlight.

Robertson Davies

Old books that have ceased to be of service should no more be abandoned than should old friends who have ceased to give pleasure.

Bernard M. Baruch

At 76, there is nothing nicer than nodding off while reading. Going fast asleep, then being woken up by the crash of the book on the floor, then saying to myself, well it doesn't matter much. An admirable feeling.

A. J. P. Taylor

Think what a better world it would be if we all, the whole world, had cookies and milk about three o'clock every afternoon and then lay down on our blankets for a nap.

Barbara Jordan

A nap in the middle of the day can do you good. If you wake up in your pyjamas – it's morning. If you're in your clothes – it's time for tea.

Thora Hird

Pleasures and Perks of Growing Older

I'm getting on. I'm now equipped with a snooze button.

Denis Norden

In spite of illness, in spite even of the arch-enemy sorrow, one can remain alive long past the usual date of disintegration if one is unafraid of change, insatiable in intellectual curiosity, interested in big things, and happy in small ways.

Edith Wharton

The woman who has a gift for old age is the woman who delights in comfort. If warmth is known as the blessing it is, if your bed, your bath, your best-liked food and drink are regarded as fresh delights, then you know how to thrive when old.

Florida Scott-Maxwell

Happiness in the older years of life, like happiness in every year of life, is a matter of choice – your choice for yourself. Happiness is to trim the day to one's own mood and feeling, to raise the window-shade of your own bedroom an hour early and squander the hour in the morning sunshine, to drink your own tea from your own teacup, to practise the little wisdoms of housekeeping, to hang a picture on the wall where memories can reach out to it a dozen times a day and to sit in your kitchen and talk to your friend.

Harold Azine

Pleasures and Perks of Growing Older

I try to make each day a miniature lifetime in which I achieve something and I enjoy something.

Leslie Bricusse

If I had known when I was 21 that I should be as happy as I am now, at 70, I should have been sincerely shocked. They promised me wormwood and funeral ravens.

Christopher Isherwood

Happiness in old age is, more than anything else, preserving the privileges of privacy.

Harold Azine

During much of my life, I was anxious to be what someone else wanted me to be. Now I have given up that struggle. I am what I am.

Elizabeth Coatsworth

I love having the freedom to do what I want, when I want and not care a darn what anyone else thinks. Like the old lady in Jenny Jones' poem, 'I shall spend my pension on brandy and summer gloves,' and no one can stop me!

Lilian Howard

One pleasure attached to growing older is that many things seem to be growing younger, growing fresher and more lively than we once supposed them to be.

G. K. Chesterton

The great thing about getting older is that you don't lose all the other ages you've been.

Madeleine L'Engle

From 51 to 53 I have been happy, and would like to remind others that their turn can come, too. It is the only message worth giving.

E. M. Forster

Let us cherish and enjoy old age; for it is full of pleasure, if you know how to use it. Fruit tastes most delicious just when its season is ending.

Seneca

Pass the Port

I have been advised by the best medical authority, at my age, not to attempt to give up alcohol.

W. C. Fields

Pass the Port

I love everything that's old – old friends, old times, old manners, old books, old wine.

Oliver Goldsmith, She Stoops to Conquer

I've stopped drinking, but only while I'm asleep.

George Best

A man is a fool if he drinks before he reaches the age of 50, and a fool if he doesn't afterward.

Frank Lloyd Wright

Actually, it only takes one drink to get me loaded. Trouble is, I can't remember if it's the 13th or 14th.

George Burns

The problem with the world is that everyone is a few drinks behind.

Humphrey Bogart

I exercise strong self-control. I never drink anything stronger than gin before breakfast.

W. C. Fields

You're not drunk if you can lie on the floor without holding on.

Joe E. Lewis

I was in for 10 hours and had 40 pints – beating my previous record by 20 minutes.

George Best, on a blood transfusion for his liver transplant, not on his drinking

Always do sober what you said you'd do drunk. That will teach you to keep your mouth shut.

Ernest Hemingway

Beer is proof that God loves us and wants us to be happy.

Benjamin Franklin

I'm not a heavy drinker; I can sometimes go for hours without touching a drop.

Noël Coward

An alcoholic is anyone you don't like who drinks more than you do.

Dylan Thomas

I know I'm drinking myself to a slow death, but then I'm in no hurry.

Robert Benchley

I often sit back and think, I wish I'd done that, and find out later that I already have.

Richard Harris, describing the effects of drinking

Pass the Port

I am a drinker with writing problems.

Brendan Behan

I feel sorry for people who don't drink. They wake up in the morning and that's the best they're going to feel all day.

Dean Martin

The difference between a drunk and an alcoholic is that a drunk doesn't have to attend all those meetings.

Arthur Lewis

A tavern is a place where madness is sold by the bottle.

Jonathan Swift

One more drink and I'll be under the host.

Dorothy Parker

The problem with some people is that when they aren't drunk, they're sober.

William Butler Yeats

Beer commercials are so patriotic: 'Made the American Way.' What does that have to do with America? Is that what America stands for? Feeling sluggish and urinating frequently?

Evelyn Waugh

A woman drove me to drink and I didn't even have the decency to thank her.

W. C. Fields

Sometimes when I reflect on all the beer I drink I feel ashamed. Then I look into the glass and think about the workers in the brewery and all of their hopes and dreams. If I didn't drink this beer, they might be out of work and their dreams would be shattered. Then I say to myself, 'It is better that I drink this beer and let their dreams come true than to be selfish and worry about my liver.'

Jack Handey

I saw a notice that said 'Drink Canada Dry' and I've just started.

Brendan Behan

I formed a new group called Alcoholics Unanimous. If you don't feel like a drink, you ring another member and he comes over to persuade you.

Richard Harris

Good old days: Beer foamed and drinking water didn't.

Anon

Be wary of strong drink. It can make you shoot at tax collectors … and miss.

Robert A. Heinlein

Pass the Port

Milk is for babies. When you grow up you have to drink beer.

Arnold Schwarzenegger

Beer, it's the best damn drink in the world.

Jack Nicholson

I drink too much. The last time I gave a urine sample it had an olive in it.

Rodney Dangerfield

I believe all drunks go to heaven, because they've been through hell on Earth.

Liza Minnelli

When I was a practising alcoholic, I was unbelievable. One side effect was immense suspicion: I'd come off tour like Inspector Clouseau on acid. 'Where's this cornflake come from? It wasn't here before.'

Ozzy Osbourne

I have a rare intolerance to herbs, which means I can only drink fermented liquids, such as gin.

Julie Walters

Pick More Daisies

REGRETS

—You're now 76 years old. Do you have any regrets in life?
—Yes, I haven't had enough sex.

Interviewer and John Betjeman

My one regret in life is that I am not someone else.

Woody Allen

My greatest regret is not knowing at 30 what I knew about women at 60.

Arthur Miller

I rather regret I haven't taken more drugs. Is it too late, at 70, to try cocaine? Would it be dangerous or interesting?

Joan Bakewell

If I had my life to live over again, I'd make the same mistakes – only sooner.

Tallulah Bankhead

You know, by the time you reach my age, you've made plenty of mistakes if you've lived your life properly.

Ronald Reagan, 76

Pick More Daisies

The only thing in my life that I regret is that I once saved David Frost from drowning. I had to pull him out, otherwise nobody would have believed I didn't push him in.

Peter Cook

My only regret in life is that I did not drink more Champagne.

John Maynard Keynes

If I had my life to live over again, I would do everything the exact same way, with the possible exception of seeing the movie remake of *Lost Horizon*.

Woody Allen

If I had my life to live over, I would pick more daisies.

Nadine Stair

If I had it all to do over again, I would spend more time with my children. I would make my money before spending it. I would learn the joys of wine instead of hard liquor. I would not smoke cigarettes when I had pneumonia. I would not marry the fifth time.

John Huston

If I had my life to live over, I'd live over a saloon.

W. C. Fields

If I had to live my life over again, I'd be a plumber.

Albert Einstein

If I had my life to live over, I don't think I'd have the strength.

Flip Wilson

If I had my life to live over again, I would have cried and laughed less while watching television and more while watching life. I would have sat on the lawn with my children and not worried about grass stains. When my kids kissed me impetuously, I would not have said, 'Later. Now go get washed for dinner.' There would have been more I love yous and more I'm sorrys. I would seize every minute … look at it and really see it … live it … and never give it back.

Erma Bombeck

I regret having been so polite in the past. I'd like to trample on at least a dozen people.

Harold Brodkey

If I have my life to live over again I should form the habit of nightly composing myself to thoughts of death. There is no other practice which so intensifies life.

Muriel Spark

Pick More Daisies

Looking back, I have this to regret, that too often when I loved, I did not say so.

David Grayson

The trouble with reaching the age of 92 is that regrets for a misspent life are bound to creep in, and whenever you see me with a furrowed brow you can be sure that what is on my mind is the thought that if only I had taken up golf earlier and devoted my whole time to it instead of fooling about writing stories and things, I might have got my handicap down to under 18.

P. G. Wodehouse

As you grow older, you'll find the only things you regret are the things you didn't do.

Zachary Scott

A man is not old until regrets take the place of your dreams.

John Barrymore

I've never really learnt how to live, and I've discovered too late that life is for living.

John Reith

Never regret. If it's good, it's wonderful. It it's bad, it's experience.

Victoria Holt

Maybe all one can do is hope to end up with the right regrets.

Arthur Miller

If I Knew Then What I Know Now – So What?

Estelle Getty, title of her autobiography

Mustn't Grumble?

I was brought up to respect my elders and now I'm 87 I don't have to respect *anybody*.

George Burns

Been There, Done That, Don't Give a F★★★ What Anybody Thinks Anymore

Slogan on a senior citizen's T-shirt

I wish I loved the Human Race;
I wish I loved its silly face;
I wish I liked the way it walks;
I wish I liked the way it talks;
And when I'm introduced to one
I wish I thought What Jolly fun!

Walter Alexander Raleigh, Wishes of an Elderly Man

Mustn't Grumble?

At age 20, we worry about what others think of us; at 40, we don't care what they think of us; at 60, we discover they haven't been thinking of us at all.

Bob Hope

I don't want a flu jab. I like getting flu. It gives me something else to complain about.

David Letterman

There's no law that decrees when and when not to whinge, but you reach a certain age – 80 seems about right – when you're expected to manifest querulousness – the coffee's too hot, the boiled egg's too soft …

Clement Freud

Bloody birthdays. Bloody women. Bloody everything. Bloody hell … Bloody footmark on the carpet now. Bloody people coming in with wet shoes …

Victor Meldrew, One Foot in the Grave

Three milk stouts – and make sure there's no lipstick on the glasses.

Ena Sharples, Coronation Street

Edith Evans bought an incredibly expensive Renoir and, when a friend asked her why she had hung it so low on the wall, out of the light behind the curtain, she replied curtly, 'Because there was a hook.'

Stephen Fry

Just because I'm in a wheelchair they think they can push me around ... I coped when a bull mastiff tried to mate with my left-side tyre.

Maud Grimes, Coronation Street

Senior Citizen: Give Me My Damn Discount

Slogan on a senior citizen's T-shirt

When I was young I was frightened I might bore people. Now I'm old I am frightened they will bore me.

Ruth Adam

Many older people are not sweet old things asking for a seat on the bus; they are in many cases demanding a turn in the driver's seat.

Michael Simmons

I'm Ageing With Attitude. I am the future. We will not be crumbling ruins.

Janet Street-Porter

Mustn't Grumble?

The Devil's in her tongue, and so 'tis in most women's of her age; for when it has quitted the tail, it repairs to the upper tier.

Aphra Behn

May your shampoo get mixed up with your Preparation H and shrink your head to the size of a mushroom.

Anon

Nobody hears old people complain because people think that's all old people do. And that's because old people are gnarled and sagged and twisted into the shape of a complaint.

Edward Albee

I refused to go on that *Grumpy Old Men* programme because I said, 'If I go on, I will be grumpy about grumpy old men.'

Stephen Fry

Sometimes I wake up grumpy; other times I let him sleep.

Car bumper sticker

I'm 101 years old and at my age, honey, I can say what I want!

Bessie Delany

In passing, also, I would like to say that the first time Adam had a chance he laid the blame on a woman.

Nancy Astor

Nothing is wrong with Southern California that a rise in the ocean level wouldn't cure.

Ross MacDonald

I hate the fact that [supermarkets are] supposed to be open 24 hours. What that means is if you go at ten at night, there's only one checkout open, so it takes you just as long as if you went at four o'clock in the afternoon.

Germaine Greer, Grumpy Old Women

There are three intolerable things in life – cold coffee, lukewarm Champagne and overexcited women.

Orson Welles

My 50 years have shown me that few people know what they are talking about. I don't mean idiots that don't know. I mean everyone.

John Cleese

Every year, back comes Spring, with nasty little birds yapping their fool heads off and the ground all mucked up with plants.

Dorothy Parker

Mustn't Grumble?

The vote means nothing to women. We should be armed.

Edna O'Brien

If all economists were laid end to end, they would not reach a conclusion.

George Bernard Shaw

Midlife can bring out your angry, bitter side. You look at your latte-swilling, beeper-wearing, know-it-all teenager and think, 'For this I have stretch marks?'

Anon

I don't like small birds. They hop around so merrily outside my window, looking so innocent. But I know that secretly, they're watching my every move and plotting to beat me over the head with a large steel pipe and take my shoe.

Jack Handey

The countryside is incredibly boring. There's lots of shagging, lots of murders, lots of sarcasm, lots of treachery, and lots of bad cooking, but it's all hidden. You've got all the space and the flowers, but it's dull!

Tom Baker

If life were fair, Dan Quayle would be making a living asking 'Do you want fries with that?'

John Cleese

They'd go to the opening of an envelope. Any big occasion, they're always there. Anything for exposure. We can do without them.
Actors are unimportant.

Richard Harris

Getting old is a terrible thing, because in your head you're not … that's another reason for the grumpiness. You actually still think of yourself as 28, and you realise that people are kinda looking at you like a sad old boy. It's bloody annoying. I hate getting old.

Sir Gerry Robinson, Grumpy Old Men

There is a remarkable breakdown of taste and intelligence at Christmas time. Mature, responsible grown men wear neckties made of holly leaves and drink alcoholic beverages with raw egg yolks in them.

P.J. O'Rourke

When one door closes, another one falls on top of you.

Angus Deayton

Mustn't Grumble?

I tell you what really turns my toes up: love scenes with 68-year-old men and actresses young enough to be their granddaughter.

Mel Gibson

Potpourri. I even find the name irritating. Potpourri.

John O'Farrell, Grumpy Old Men

If you think health care is expensive now, wait until you see what it costs when it's free.

P.J. O'Rourke

The average airplane is 16 years old, and so is the average airplane meal.

Joan Rivers

If I were reincarnated, I would wish to be returned to Earth as a killer virus to lower human population levels.

Prince Philip

I have always hated that damn James Bond. I'd like to kill him.

Sean Connery

I am not over-fond of animals.

David Attenborough

I think it's quite possible that there's a government department somewhere devoted to coming up with really annoying ideas. You know, let's not have fresh milk on trains any more, let's have those little cartons of UHT because that'll piss everyone off.

John O'Farrell, Grumpy Old Men

I have a total irreverence for anything connected with society except that which makes the roads safer, the beer stronger, the food cheaper and the old men and old women warmer in the winter and happier in the summer.

Brendan Behan

Why does a person even get up in the morning? You have breakfast, you floss your teeth so you'll have healthy gums in your old age, and then you get in your car and drive down I-10 and die. Life is so stupid I can't stand it.

Barbara Kingsolver

Progress might have been all right once, but it has gone on too long.

Ogden Nash

I wish people who have trouble communicating would just shut up.

Tom Lehrer

Mustn't Grumble?

The surprising thing about young fools is how many survive to become old fools.

Doug Larson

I can win an argument on any topic, against any opponent. People know this, and steer clear of me at parties. Often, as a sign of their great respect, they don't even invite me.

Dave Barry

I don't have pet peeves, I have whole kennels of irritation.

Whoopi Goldberg

If life was fair, Elvis would be alive and all the impersonators would be dead.

Johnny Carson

I don't like animals. It's a strange thing. I don't like men and I don't like animals. As for God, he is beginning to disgust me.

Samuel Beckett

I hate women because they always know where things are.

James Thurber

If the English language made any sense, a catastrophe would be an apostrophe with fur.

Doug Larson

Think of how stupid the average person is, and realise half of them are stupider than that.

George Carlin

Santa Claus has the right idea. Visit people only once a year.

Victor Borge

Few things are more satisfying than seeing your own children have teenagers of their own.

Doug Larson

I don't like the word 'superstar'. It has ridiculous implications. These words – star, stupor, superstar, stupid star – they're misleading. It's a myth.

Barbra Streisand

I am so busy doing nothing … that the idea of doing anything – which as you know, always leads to something – cuts into the nothing and then forces me to have to drop everything.

Jerry Seinfeld

Mustn't Grumble?

I'm getting fed up of living away from home so much. They look after you very well but it doesn't matter how well you're looked after, how nice the hotel is: if you're away from home constantly, the bloody dog savages you, thinks you're a stranger, the kid cries and the wife's stuck to your face!

David Jason

USA Today has come out with a new survey: apparently three out of four people make up 75 per cent of the population.

David Letterman

Women speak because they wish to speak, whereas a man speaks only when driven to speech by something outside himself – like, for instance, he can't find any clean socks.

Jean Kerr

Now they show you how detergents take out bloodstains – a pretty violent image there. I think if you've got a T-shirt with a bloodstain all over it, maybe laundry isn't your biggest problem. Maybe you should get rid of the body before you do the wash.

Jerry Seinfeld

Rock journalism is people who can't write interviewing people who can't talk for people who can't read.

Frank Zappa

If the world should blow itself up, the last audible voice would be that of an expert saying it can't be done.

Peter Ustinov

I think on-stage nudity is disgusting, shameful and damaging to all things American. But if I were 22 with a great body, it would be artistic, tasteful, patriotic and a progressive religious experience.

Shelley Winters

Man invented language to satisfy his deep need to complain.

Lily Tomlin

The days of the digital watch are numbered.

Tom Stoppard

A healthy male adult bore consumes each year one and a half times his own weight in other people's patience.

John Updike

I'm convinced there's a small room in the attic of the Foreign Office where future diplomats are taught to stammer.

Peter Ustinov

A lot of people like snow. I find it to be an unnecessary freezing of water.

Carl Reiner

An intellectual snob is someone who can listen to the William Tell Overture and not think of *The Lone Ranger*.

Dan Rather

The Trouble Today Is...

We live in an age when pizza gets to your home before the police.

Jeff Marder

Everything is drive-through. In California, they even have a burial service called Jump-In-The-Box.

Wil Shriner

It's easy to identify people who can't count to 10. They're in front of you in the supermarket express lane.

M. Grundler

The trouble with our times is that the future is not what it used to be.

Paul Valéry

Too bad that all the people who know how to run the country are driving taxi cabs and cutting hair.

George Burns

The trouble with being punctual is that nobody's there to appreciate it.

Franklin P. Jones

I get furious with people who don't serve me immediately, if I think they're not doing anything. If they're sort of closing drawers or checking lists or something, and they don't serve me immediately. I want to kill them. I want to leap over and throttle them.

Dillie Keane, Grumpy Old Women

The rage that happens in shops happens, normally, because of bad service. There's appalling service in Britain. Appalling. I mean unimaginably dire service, and we all put up with it.

India Knight, Grumpy Old Women

The Trouble Today Is...

I am amazed at radio DJs today. I am firmly convinced that AM on my radio stands for Absolute Moron. I will not begin to tell you what FM stands for.

Jasper Carrott

We've all seen them, on the street corners, many of them smoking, many of them on drugs; they've got no jobs to go to, and once a week we see them queuing for the state hand-outs – or pensions, as we call them.

Harry Hill

What about safety matches? I never get that. What is a safety match? What does that mean? It's a box of matches you could ignite; you could burn a house down.

Nigel Havers, Grumpy Old Men

All my life I have sneered at the old farts who said that the world is going to the dogs, and at last I have realised, my God, they are right.

Jan Morris

Waiters and waitresses are becoming nicer and more caring. I used to pay my cheque, they would say, 'Thank you.' That's now escalated into, 'You take care of yourself, now.' The other day I paid my cheque and the waiter said, 'Don't put off that mammogram.'

Rita Rudner

...that it is all signpost and no destination.

Louis Kronenberger

The youth of the present day are quite monstrous. They have absolutely no respect for dyed hair.

Oscar Wilde

Newspapers are unable, seemingly, to discriminate between a bicycle accident and the collapse of civilisation.

George Bernard Shaw

You can say this for ready-mixes – the next generation isn't going to have any trouble making pies exactly like mother used to make.

Earl Wilson

We are living in a world today where lemonade is made from artificial flavours and furniture polish is made from real lemons.

Alfred E. Newman

You can find your way across this country using burger joints the way a navigator uses stars.

Charles Kuralt

The Trouble Today Is...

Few cultures have not produced the idea that in some past era the world ran better than it does now.

Elizabeth Janeway

Now there are more overweight people in America than average-weight people. So overweight people are now average. Which means you've met your New Year's resolution.

Jay Leno

Pol Pot killed 1.7 million Cambodians, died under house arrest, well done there. Stalin killed many millions, died in his bed, aged 72, well done indeed. And the reason we let them get away with it is they killed their own people. And we're sort of fine with that. Hitler killed people next door. Oh, stupid man. After a couple of years we won't stand for that, will we?

Eddie Izzard

What some people mistake for the high cost of living is really the cost of high living.

Doug Larson

Nowadays men lead lives of noisy desperation.

James Thurber

If God had wanted us to vote, he would have given us candidates.

Jay Leno

The trouble with political jokes is that very often they get elected.

Will Rogers

The White House is giving George W. Bush intelligence briefings. You know, some of these jokes just write themselves.

David Letterman

My husband gave me a necklace. It's fake. I requested fake. Maybe I'm paranoid, but in this day and age, I don't want something around my neck that's worth more than my head.

Rita Rudner

Another possible source of guidance for teenagers is television, but television's message has always been that the need for truth, wisdom and world peace pales by comparison with the need for a toothpaste that offers whiter teeth and fresher breath.

Dave Barry

The Trouble Today Is...

For the first time in history, sex is more dangerous than the cigarette afterward.

Jay Leno

I loathe the expression 'What makes him tick.' It is the American mind, looking for simple and singular solution, that uses the foolish expression. A person not only ticks, he also chimes and strikes the hour, falls and breaks and has to be put together again, and sometimes stops like an electric clock in a thunderstorm.

James Thurber

Politics: 'Poli', a Latin word meaning 'many'; and 'tics' meaning 'bloodsucking creatures'.

Robin Williams

Thus the metric system did not really catch on in the States, unless you count the increasing popularity of the nine-millimetre bullet.

Dave Barry

What the world needs is more geniuses with humility; there are so few of us left.

Oscar Levant

A common mistake people make when trying to design something completely foolproof is to underestimate the ingenuity of complete fools.

Douglas Adams

I have six locks on my door all in a row. When I go out, I only lock every other one. I figure no matter how long somebody stands there picking the locks, they are always locking three.

Elayne Boosler

It's amazing that the amount of news that happens in the world every day always just exactly fits the newspaper.

Jerry Seinfeld

For every fatal shooting, there were roughly three non-fatal shootings. And, folks, this is unacceptable in America. It's just unacceptable. And we're going to do something about it.

George W. Bush

Last week I was walking by a cemetery, two guys came after me with shovels. It was all about money.

Rodney Dangerfield

The streets are safe in Philadelphia. It's only the people who make them unsafe.

Frank Rizzo, ex-police chief and mayor of Philadelphia

Americans will put up with anything provided it doesn't block traffic.

Dan Rather

A bookstore is one of the only pieces of evidence we have that people are still thinking.

Jerry Seinfeld

Menopause

Is It Me Or Is It Hot in Here? A Modern Woman's Guide to the Menopause

Jenni Murray, book title

The menopause is the stage that woman goes through when her body, through a complex biological process, senses that the woman has reached the stage in her life where her furniture is much too nice for her to have a baby barfing on it.

Dave Barry

—Oh my God, Saffy, darling, help. I'm having a hot flush. I don't believe it. It's a hot flush. Feel my skin.
—Mum, you're standing too close to the kettle.

Edina and Saffron Monsoon, Absolutely Fabulous

Someone told me that giving up chocolate would reduce my hot flushes. To be honest, I prefer the hot flushes.

Anna Granger

I like the hot flushes. It's like being in love again without the aggravation.

Joy Behar

Real women don't have hot flushes, they have power surges.

Car bumper sticker

It's the menopause. I've got my own climate.

Julie Walters

I went to see my doctor to talk to him about this menopause thing, because I don't know if I really want to do it.

Jane Condon

Menopause

A friend of mine, Norma Cowles, started The Change at Pontins in Torquay but there were absolutely no menopausal facilities there whatsoever. Something for Judith Chalmers to think about.

Mrs Merton

My grandma told me, 'The good news is, after menopause the hair on your legs gets really thin and you don't have to shave anymore. Which is great because it means you have more time to work on your new moustache.'

Karen Haber

I refuse to think of them as chin hairs. I think of them as stray eyebrows.

Janette Barber

I'm trying very hard to understand the younger generation. They have adjusted the timetable for childbearing so that menopause and teaching a 16-year-old how to drive a car will occur in the same week.

Erma Bombeck

Why did the menopausal woman cross the road? To kill the chicken.

Jane Condon

YOU KNOW YOU'RE MENOPAUSAL WHEN...

...you're adding chocolate chips to your cheese omelette.

...the dryer has shrunk every last pair of your jeans.

...everyone around you has an attitude problem.

...your husband is suddenly agreeing to everything you say.

...you're using your cellular phone to dial up every bumper sticker that says 'How's my driving – call 1-800-***-.'

...everyone's head looks like an invitation to batting practice.

...you're convinced there's a God and he's male.

...you can't believe they don't make a tampon bigger than Super Plus.

...you're sure that everyone is scheming to drive you crazy.

...the ibuprofen bottle is empty and you bought it yesterday.

All Anonymous

Menopause

Male menopause is a lot more fun than female menopause. With female menopause you gain weight and get hot flashes. Male menopause – you get to date young girls and drive motorcycles.

Rita Rudner

I do get hot. Sometimes I think, 'Oh I can smell the menopause on me.' You know, it's kind of BO and Prozac and furniture polish.

Jenny Eclair, Grumpy Old Women

My first day as a woman and I am already having hot flushes.

Robin Williams, Mrs Doubtfire

Middle-aged men are fine if they accept that they're middle-aged men. In fact, they're rather interesting when they accept that they're middle-aged men. But when they decide that they're going to act as if they're 19 or 20, and dress in a style that is inappropriate to that age, then it really is pathetic.

Ann Widdecombe, Grumpy Old Women

Rock and menopause do not mix. It is not good, it sucks and every day I fight it to the death, or, at the very least, not let it take me over.

Stevie Nicks

Menopause

Charlotte: Listen to this: sometime in the 10 years before menopause, you may experience symptoms including all-month-long PMS, fluid retention, insomnia, depression, hot flashes or irregular periods.
Carrie: On the plus side, people start to give up their seats for you on the bus.

Sex and the City

Inevitably I'm being given a hard time for being a typical ageing male, going off and packing in the wife.

Rick Stein

For my sister's 50th birthday, I sent her a singing mammogram.

Steven Wright

I'm out of oestrogen and I've got a gun!

Bumper sticker

The seven dwarves of menopause; itchy, bitchy, sweaty, sleepy, bloated, forgetful and psycho.

Anon

I'm developing a new fondness for Michael Douglas, now that he's getting all menopausal and wrinkly.

John Patterson

I certainly hope I'm not still answering child-star questions by the time I reach menopause.

Christina Ricci

At Least I Have My Health

I've just become a pensioner so I've started saving up for my own hospital trolley.

Tom Baker

The time will come in your life, it will almost certainly come, when the voice of God will thunder at you from a cloud, 'From this day forth thou shalt not be able to put on thine own socks.'

John Mortimer

I feel age like an icicle down my back.

Dyson Carter

When I wake up in the morning and nothing hurts, I know I must be dead.

George Burns

I don't need you to remind me of my age. I have a bladder to do that for me.

Stephen Fry

At Least I Have My Health

When you get to my age, life seems little more than one long march to and from the lavatory.

John Mortimer

At 75, I sleep like a log. I never have to get up in the middle of the night to go to the bathroom. I go in the morning. Every morning, like clockwork, at 7am, I pee. Unfortunately, I don't wake up till 8.

Harry Beckworth

Thanks to modern medical advances such as antibiotics, nasal spray and Diet Coke, it has become routine for people in the civilised world to pass the age of 40, sometimes more than once.

Dave Barry

When I was 40, my doctor advised me that a man in his 40s shouldn't play tennis. I heeded his advice carefully and could hardly wait until I reached 50 to start again.

Hugo Black

When I turned 50, I went off to have my prostate checked because I kept reading I should. Fucking finger up the arse, I can do without that again.

Bob Geldof

At Least I Have My Health

Be suspicious of any doctor who tries to take your temperature with his finger.

David Letterman

—How do you know which pills to take?
—Doesn't make any difference. Whatever they fix, I got.

Oscar Madison and Felix Ungar, The Odd Couple II

My mother is no spring chicken, although she has got as many chemicals in her as one.

Dame Edna Everage

Why do the medical profession still keep writing on prescription bottles in a size that only a 20-year-old can read? You were standing there with the medicine bottle in your hand and you died because you couldn't read the directions.

Bill Cosby

Half the modern drugs could well be thrown out the window, except that the birds might eat them.

Martin H. Fischer

I don't know much about medicine, but I know what I like.

S. J. Perelman

Casey came home from seeing the doctor looking very worried. His wife said, 'What's the problem?' He said, 'The doctor told me I have to take a pill every day for the rest of my life.' She said, 'So what? Lots of people have to take a pill every day for the rest of their lives.' He said, 'I know, but he only gave me four.'

Hal Roach

The good Lord never gives you more than you can handle. Unless you die of something.

Steve Martin

You're 50 years old! Can they make a drug to help you through all of that, to keep all your organs intact until your golden years? No. Can they make a drug to give mental clarity to your golden time? No. What they've got is Viagra, a drug to make you harder than Chinese algebra.

Robin Williams

The doctor said, 'I have good news and bad news. The good news is: you're not a hypochondriac.'

Bob Monkhouse

The doctor said to me, 'You're going to live till you're 60.' I said, 'I am 60.' He said, 'What did I tell you?'

Henny Youngman

At Least I Have My Health

When you get to my age, getting a second doctor's opinion is like switching slot machines.

James Walker

Now I'm over 50 my doctor says I should go out and get more fresh air and exercise. I said, 'All right, I'll drive with the car window open.'

Angus Walker

How can people complain about the length of time spent waiting in Out Patients for an appointment? I've spent many happy hours in our local hospital familiarizing myself with people's ailments and afflictions.

Mrs Merton

Whoever thought up the word 'Mammogram'? Every time I hear it, I think I'm supposed to put my breast in an envelope and send it to someone.

Jan King

Everyone goes into an aeroplane or a hospital wondering if they'll ever get out of either alive.

Richard Gordon

I was under the care of a couple of medical students who couldn't diagnose a decapitation.

Jeffrey Bernard

At Least I Have My Health

There's nothing wrong with you that an expensive operation can't prolong.

Graham Chapman

The NHS don't think of it as having lost a patient, more as having gained a bed.

Anon

He's on the mend, sitting up in bed blowing the froth off his medicine.

Flann O'Brien

Getting out of the hospital is a lot like resigning from a book club. You're not out of it until the computer says you're out of it.

Erma Bombeck

I rang the Enema Helpline. They were very rude.

Jack Dee

Always keep tubes of haemorrhoid ointment and Deep Heat rub well separated in your bathroom cabinet.

P. Turner, Top Tip, Viz

I'm at an age where my back goes out more than I do.

Phyllis Diller

At Least I Have My Health

No one should grow old who isn't ready to appear ridiculous.

John Mortimer

You don't know real embarrassment until your hip sets off a metal detector.

Ross McGuiness

One of the most embarrassing moments when you get to my age is to have to urinate under pressure with a line behind you. I step up to the urinal full of dreams of instant relief, only to find my body saying, 'Why are we here?'

Bill Cosby

1960s VERSUS 1990s …

Then: getting into a new hip joint
Now: getting a new hip joint

Then: long hair
Now: longing for hair

Then: killer weed
Now: weedkiller

Then: taking acid
Now: taking antacid

Then: trying to look like Elizabeth Taylor
Now: trying not to look like Elizabeth Taylor

Anon

Growing old brings some disadvantages, like you start having trouble with the coconut ones in Liquorice Allsorts; bending over becomes a major decision; and you can't count the number of times a day you find yourself moving in one direction when you should be moving in the other.

Denis Norden

Of all the self-fulfilling prophecies in our culture, the assumption that ageing means decline and poor health is probably the deadliest.

Marilyn Ferguson

Age is a product of good health. Our research shows that people who live to be 100 are as mentally and physically healthy as people 30 years younger. We've replaced the saying, 'The older you get, the sicker you get', with the more accurate, 'The older you get, the healthier you've been'.

Dr Thomas Perls

There are many mysteries in old age, but the greatest, surely, is this: in those adverts for walk-in bathtubs, why doesn't all the water gush out when you get in?

Alan Coren

At Least I Have My Health

Have you seen the afternoon telly they put on for poor old crocks and old-age-perishers? You're just dozing off to a black-and-white film starring James Mason when he was in short trousers, when on comes that chap from *All Creatures Great and Small* saying, 'Have you thought about your funeral?' Then on comes some old girl whizzing up and down stairs on a stairlift. It's all based on fear and meant to scare you.

Ken Dodd

We have put more effort into helping folks reach old age than into helping them enjoy it.

Frank A. Clark

My wife's aunt is about 109 years old and has a pair of glasses for every activity you can imagine – glasses for knitting, glasses for reading, glasses for doing the crossword. But she's always losing them. 'Have you seen my glasses?' she'll say. 'Surely you have a pair of looking-for-your-glasses glasses, don't you?'

Jack Dee

It's extraordinary. My mother doesn't need glasses at all and here I am 52, 56 – well, whatever age I am – and can't see a thing.

Queen Elizabeth II

My grandmother is over 80 and still doesn't need glasses. Drinks right out of the bottle.

Henny Youngman

I prefer to forget both pairs of glasses and pass my declining years saluting strange women and grandfather clocks.

Ogden Nash

From the age of 75 on, I have found my memory deteriorating and my senses getting less acute. I can mistake a reference to 'Stena Sealink' on television for 'Denis Healey'.

Denis Healey

My dad became more and more deaf, relying on lip-reading to understand people, and almost to spite him, my mother became a Moslem Fundamentalist.

Harry Hill

My granny wore a hearing aid that was always tuned too low. Because when she turned it up, it whistled, and every dog in Dublin rushed to her side.

Terry Wogan

When I turn my hearing aid up to 10, I can hear a canary break wind six miles away.

Sophia Petrillo, The Golden Girls

At Least I Have My Health

My grandmother was insane. She had pierced hearing aids.

Steven Wright

I had a job selling hearing aids door to door. It wasn't easy, because your best prospects never answered.

Bob Monkhouse

It's been said that if you're not radical at 20, you have no heart; if you're still radical at 40, you have no brain. Of course, either way, at 60 you usually have no teeth.

Bill Maher

—Dorothy, have you seen my teeth?
—They're in your mouth, Ma.
—I know that. Don't they look good today? I ran them through the dishwasher.

Sophia Petrillo and Dorothy Zbornak, The Golden Girls

My 92-year-old aunt, in hospital to have a pacemaker fitted, was asked by the nurse preparing her for the operation: 'Please give me your teeth.' 'Certainly not,' was her stern reply. She still has her own.

Roger Lines

At Least I Have My Health

I visited a new dentist for my six-monthly check-up. Having given me the all-clear, he glanced at my notes, then remarked: 'Those should see you out.'

Angela Walder, 72

From the bathroom came the sound of my grandmother brushing her tooth.

Peter de Vries

My father kept several pairs of false teeth, one set in a jar marked 'Best Pair', another marked 'Next Best' and a third marked 'Not Bad'.

David Hockney

My friend George has false teeth – with braces on them.

Steven Wright

When you're my age, you just never risk being ill – because then everyone says, 'Oh, he's done for.'

John Gielgud

You will die not because you are ill. You will die because you are alive.

Seneca

At Least I Have My Health

Never talk about yourself as being old. There is something in Mind Cure, after all, and, if you continually talk of yourself as being old, you may perhaps bring on some of the infirmities of age.

Hannah Smith

No one sophisticated, glamorous or interesting over 60 talks about age. So why then do other people react to life after 60 as though it were a sludge-coloured blanket which they've pulled defiantly around them crocheted large with the word 'OLD'?

Marcelle D'Argy-Smith

Old age means a crown of thorns, and the trick is to wear it jauntily.

Christopher Morley

Eighty years old! No eyes left, no ears, no teeth, no legs, no wind! And when all is said and done, how astonishingly well one does without them!

Paul Claudel

Use your health, even to the point of wearing it out. That is what it is for. Spend all you have before you die; do not outlive yourself.

George Bernard Shaw

At Least I Have My Health

I'm not to blame for an old body, but I would be to blame for an old soul. An old soul is a shameful thing.

Margaret Deland

First the doctor told me the good news: I was going to have a disease named after me.

Steve Martin

My father died of cancer when I was a teenager. He had it before it became popular.

Goodman Ace

You know you're getting old when everything hurts. And what doesn't hurt doesn't work.

Hy Gardner

The trouble with heart disease is that the first symptom is often hard to deal with: sudden death.

Michael Phelps

I am afraid … that health begins, after 70, and often long before, to have a meaning different from that which it had at 30. But it is culpable to murmur at the established order of the creation, as it is vain to oppose it. He that lives, must grow old; and he that would rather grow old than die, has God to thank for the infirmities of old age.

Samuel Johnson

At Least I Have My Health

My doctor gave me six months to live, but when I couldn't pay the bill he gave me six more.

Walter Matthau

Life begins at 40 – but so do fallen arches, rheumatism, faulty eyesight, and the tendency to tell a story to the same person three or four times.

William Feather

As the arteries grow hard, the heart grows soft.

Henry Louis Mencken

Nobody expects to trust his body over-much after the age of 50.

Edward Hoagland

The trouble about always trying to preserve the health of the body is that it is so difficult to do without destroying the health of the mind.

G. K. Chesterton

Two elderly gentlemen from a retirement centre were sitting on a bench under a tree when one turned to the other and said, 'Ted, I'm 83 years old now and I'm just full of aches and pains. I know you're about my age. How do you feel?'

Ted said, 'I feel like a newborn baby.'

'Really? Like a newborn baby?'

'Yep. No hair, no teeth, and I think I just wet my pants.'

Anon

I drive way too fast to worry about cholesterol.

Steven Wright

We all get heavier as we get older because there is a lot more information in our heads.

Vlade Divac

The spiritual eyesight improves as the physical eyesight declines.

Plato

Don't you think it's unnerving that doctors call what they do 'Practice'?

George Carlin

Quit worrying about your health. It'll go away.

Robert Orben

Each year it grows harder to make ends meet – the ends I refer to are hands and feet.

Richard Armour

At Least I Have My Health

It's no longer a question of staying healthy. It's a question of finding a sickness you like.

Jackie Mason

A woman walked up to a little old man rocking in a chair on his porch.

'I couldn't help noticing how happy you look,' she said. 'What's your secret for a long, happy life?'

'I smoke three packs of cigarettes a day,' he said. 'I also drink a case of whisky a week, eat fatty foods, and never exercise.'

'That's amazing,' the woman said. 'How old are you?'

'Twenty-six,' he said.

Anon

Never under any circumstances take a sleeping pill and a laxative on the same night.

Dave Barry

So who's perfect? Washington had false teeth. Franklin was nearsighted. Mussolini had syphilis. Unpleasant things have been said about Walt Whitman and Oscar Wilde. Tchaikovsky had his problems, too. And Lincoln was constipated.

John O'Hara

At Least I Have My Health

I have finally come to the conclusion that a good, reliable set of bowels is worth more to man than any quantity of brains.

Josh Billings

My grandfather is hard of hearing. He needs to read lips. I don't mind him reading lips, but he uses one of those yellow highlighters.

Brian Kiley

A man does not die of love or his liver or even of old age; he dies of being a man.

Percival Arland Ussher

I think most people would pick sudden heart attack and in sleep. We assume that's the best way to die, because you never know.

Jack Kevorkian

There are only three things that can kill a farmer: lightning, rolling over in a tractor, and old age.

Bill Bryson

For years I was an undiagnosed anorexic, suffering from a little-known variant of the disease, where, freakishly, the appetite turns in on itself and demands more and more food, forcing the sufferer to gain several stones in weight and wear men's V-necked pullovers. My condition has stabilised now, but I can never stray too far from cocoa-based products and I keep a small cracknel-type candy in my brassiere at all times. Fortunately, I wear a 'D' cup so there is plenty of room for sweetmeats…

Victoria Wood

I feel stronger, but physically I feel like I'm falling apart. Every day I get a new pain or ache and think, 'Oh, that will be a hip replacement in a couple of years!'

Yasmin Le Bon

Money cannot buy health, but I'd settle for a diamond-studded wheelchair.

Dorothy Parker

I think that in youth you never view an ailment as possibly fatal. When you get an ailment in middle age, you are automatically planning your own funeral…

Will Self

I have such poor vision I can date anybody.

Garry Shandling

Doctor, Doctor

THE MEDICAL PROFESSION

In the name of Hippocrates, doctors have invented the most exquisite form of torture ever known to man: survival.

Luis Buñuel

Cured yesterday of my disease, I died last night of my physician.

Matthew Prior

The medics can now stretch life out an additional dozen years but they don't tell you that most of these years are going to be spent flat on your back while some ghoul with thick glasses and a matted skull peers at you through a machine that's hot out of 'Space Patrol'.

Groucho Marx

Beware of the young doctor and the old barber.

Benjamin Franklin

The doctor called Mrs Cohen, saying, 'Mrs Cohen, your cheque came back.' Mrs Cohen answered, 'So did my arthritis!' The doctor says, 'You'll live to be 60!' 'I AM 60!' 'See, what did I tell you?'

Henny Youngman

Doctor, Doctor

Too many good docs are getting out of the business. Too many OB-GYNs aren't able to practise their love with women all across this country.

George W. Bush

My doctor is wonderful. Once, in 1955, when I couldn't afford an operation, he touched up the X-rays.

Joey Bishop

After two days in hospital, I took a turn for the nurse.

W. C. Fields

Doctors are the same as lawyers; the only difference is that lawyers merely rob you, whereas doctors rob you and kill you, too.

Anton Chekhov

One of the most difficult things to contend with in a hospital is that assumption on the part of the staff that because you have lost your gall-bladder you have also lost your mind.

Jean Kerr

Keep away from physicians. It is all probing and guessing and pretending with them. They leave it to Nature to cure in her own time, but they take the credit. As well as very fat fees.

Anthony Burgess

My doctor tells me I'm in very good nick. The most positive way to think about death is to try to live.

Michael Caine

The ultimate indignity is to be given a bedpan by a stranger who calls you by your first name.

Maggie Kuhn

I'm not feeling very well, I need a doctor immediately. Ring the nearest golf course.

Groucho Marx

Thanks to modern medicine we are no longer forced to endure prolonged pain, disease, discomfort and wealth.

Robert Orben

At my age, every doctor says the same thing: it's either something I have to live with – or something I have to live without.

Anon

Never go to a doctor whose office plants have died.

Erma Bombeck

My doctor gave me two weeks to live. I hope they are in August.

Ronnie Shakes

Doctor, Doctor

Our doctor would never really operate unless it was necessary. He was just that way. If he didn't need the money, he wouldn't lay a hand on you.

Herb Shriner

My doctor once said to me, 'Do you think I'm here for the good of your health?'

Bob Monkhouse

America's health care system is second only to Japan … Canada, Sweden, Great Britain … well, all of Europe. But you can thank your lucky stars we don't live in Paraguay!

Homer Simpson

A hospital bed is a parked taxi with the meter running.

Groucho Marx

A woman tells her doctor, 'I've got a bad back.' The doctor says, 'It's old age.' The woman says, 'I want a second opinion.' The doctor says: 'Okay – you're ugly as well.'

Tommy Cooper

My kid could get a bad X-ray and I could get a call from the doctor saying I have something growing in my bum and that would change my perspective on everything instantaneously, on what is and what is not important.

Tom Hanks

I've wrestled with reality for 35 years, and I'm happy, Doctor. I finally won out over it.

Jimmy Stewart, Harvey

Dick Cheney said he was running again. He said his health was fine: 'I've got a doctor with me 24 hours a day.' Yeah, that's always the sign of a man in good health, isn't it?

David Letterman

I kept thinking about that large doctor, sweaty, who brought my mother home after the first heart attack. He said, 'Don't ever get angry at your mother – that might kill her.' That set off my demons, I think.

Gene Wilder

I told the doctor I broke my leg in two places. He told me to quit going to those places.

Henny Youngman

Dad always thought laughter was the best medicine, which I guess is why several of us died of tuberculosis.

Jack Handey

Doctor, Doctor

I don't know why people question the academic training of an athlete. Fifty per cent of the doctors in this country graduated in the bottom half of their classes.

Al McGuire

When I go in for a physical, they no longer ask how old I am. They just carbon-date me.

Ronald Reagan

There's a new medical crisis. Doctors are reporting that many men are having allergic reactions to latex condoms. They say they cause severe swelling. So what's the problem?

Dustin Hoffman

I know of nothing more laughable than a doctor who does not die of old age.

Voltaire

On a Friday night it's like a field hospital in the Battle of the Somme. There's blokes with blood coming out of their heads and Bacardi Breezer bottles stuck in their necks.

John O'Farrell, on A&E departments in Grumpy Old Men

No Medical, and No Salesman Will Call

INSURANCE

What would make life better for old people? Axe that Churchill Insurance 'nodding dog' commercial on television.

Clement Freud

All big stars of my parents' generation are on cable TV selling things. Insurance policies to the elderly, asking them to send in $7.95 out of their last eight dollars for a policy that will leave money to children who don't visit them.

Louie Anderson

Life insurance is a weird concept. You really don't get anything for it. It works like this: you pay me money and when you die, I'll pay you money.

Bill Kirchenbauer

There are worse things in life than death. Have you ever spent an evening with an insurance salesman?

Woody Allen

I detest life-insurance agents; they always argue that I shall some day die, which is not so.

Stephen Leacock

I took a physical for some life insurance. All they would give me was fire and theft.

Milton Berle

I have done many insurance physical check-ups on people and as far as I can tell, an insurance physical can only determine one thing – whether or not you are going to die during the physical.

Dr Mark DePaolis

My wife and I took out life insurance policies on one another, so now it's just a waiting game.

Bill Dwyer

Going Gaga

They say that after the age of 20 you lose 50,000 brain cells a day. I don't believe it. I think it's much more.

Ned Sherrin

A 'senior moment' is a euphemism to indicate a temporary loss of marbles to anyone over 50.

Anon

As you get older, you've probably noticed that you tend to forget things. You'll be talking at a party, and you'll know that you know this person, but no matter how hard you try, you can't remember his or her name. This can be very embarrassing, especially if he or she turns out to be your spouse.

Dave Barry

Remembering something at first try is now as good as an orgasm as far as I'm concerned.

Gloria Steinem

First, you forget names, then you forget faces. Next, you forget to pull your zipper up and finally you forget to pull it down.

Leo Rosenberg

My memory's starting to go. The only thing I still retain is water.

Alex Cole

To my deafness I'm accustomed,
To my dentures I'm resigned,
I can manage my bifocals,
But O, how I miss my mind.

Anon

—Hurry up, Dorothy, we're going to be late for Temple.
—Ma, it's Tuesday and we're Catholic.

Sophia Petrillo and Dorothy Zbornak, The Golden Girls

Going Gaga

'You are old, Father William,' the young man said,
'And your hair has become very white;
And yet you incessantly stand on your head –
Do you think, at your age, it is right?'
'In my youth,' Father William replied to his son,
'I feared it might injure the brain;
But, now that I'm perfectly sure I have none,
Why, I do it again and again.'

Lewis Carroll

I had always looked on myself as a sort of freak whom age could not touch, which was where I made the ruddy error, because I'm really a senile wreck with about one and a half feet in the grave.

P. G. Wodehouse, 69

His golf bag doesn't contain a full set of irons.

Robin Williams

I still have a full deck. I just shuffle slower.

Milton Berle

Spare a thought for my friend Eliza Hamilton, who was wrongly diagnosed as mentally unstable when all she was was a bit giddy.

Mrs Merton

The Mayoress was visiting an old folk's home. As she went round she saw an old lady sitting there, and said to her, brightly, 'Good morning.' The old lady looked a bit puzzled, so the Mayoress said, 'Do you know who I am?' The old lady gave her a sympathetic look and said, 'No, dear, but if you ask the matron, she'll tell you.'

Anon

Been There, Done That, Can't Remember.

Slogan on a senior citizen's T-shirt

—Can you remember any of your past lives?
—At my age I have a problem remembering what happened yesterday.

Interviewer and the Dalai Lama

The face is familiar, but I can't remember my name.

Robert Benchley

At my age, you learn a new name, you gotta forget an old one.

Wesley Birdsong, Lone Star

That phrase they use, 'in living memory' – as in 'the worst floods in living memory' or 'the coldest winter in living memory' – just how far back does it stretch?

Going Gaga

Because at my age, my 'living memory' goes back to a week last Tuesday.

Alan Coren

I remember things that happened 60 years ago, but if you ask me where I left my car keys five minutes ago, that's sometimes a problem.

Lou Thesz

When I was younger I could remember anything, whether it happened or not, but I am getting old and now that I am 71 I shall soon remember only the latter.

Mark Twain

All the failures of memory that can plague you, such as losing your car at the mall or losing your glasses on your forehead or losing the reason you entered a room, are minor when compared to the most embarrassing trick your mind can play: forgetting what you've been talking about. How come I can remember events of 30 years ago but not what I said in the last 30 seconds?

Bill Cosby

I know a lot of old people. They're all the same. They're cranky. They're demanding. They repeat themselves. They're cranky.

Sophia Petrillo, The Golden Girls

They will all have heard that story of yours before – but if you tell it well they won't mind hearing it again.

Thora Hird

My grandmother's 85 and starting to get forgetful. The family's upset about it but I don't mind because I get eight cheques on my birthday from her. That's 40 bucks.

Tom Arnold

You remind me of a poem I can't remember, and a song that may never have existed, and a place I'm not sure I've ever been to.

Grandpa Simpson, The Simpsons

—We met at nine.
—We met at eight.
—I was on time.
—No, you were late.
—Ah yes, I remember it well.

Maurice Chevalier and Hermione Gingold, Gigi

I'm very old – in my 90th year. I have a horrible dislike of old age. Everybody's dead – half, no nearly all of one's contemporaries – and those that aren't are gaga. Someone rang the other day and said, 'I want to invite you and Duff over for dinner.' I said, 'But Duff's been dead for 28 years.' [taps her forehead] That's what I dread.

Lady Diana Cooper

Going Gaga

Body and mind, like man and wife, do not always agree to die together.

Peter Ouspensky

My mother is 96, and had a bad fall and a blackout a few days ago. The doctor who examined her in the A&E clearly thought she was a bit gaga, so asked her to count down from 20. 'Better than that,' she said, 'I'll do it in French,' and got down to 'douze' before the doctor, chastened, said, 'OK, OK.'

David Horchover

They tell you that you'll lose your mind when you grow older. What they don't tell you is that you won't miss it very much.

Malcolm Cowley

I'm not worried about senility. My grandfather said, 'When you become senile, you won't know it.'

Bill Cosby

I am in the prime of senility.

Joel C. Harris

I'm not senile. I've been like this for 50 years. So even if I do become senile, people will never know.

Martin Landis, Night Court

As you get older three things happen. The first is your memory goes, and I can't remember the other two.

Sir Norman Wisdom

I believe the true function of age is memory. I'm recording as fast as I can.

Rita Mae Brown

Just sometimes you bump into people and you think, 'You're my best friend, aren't you? I recognise you. Ooh, you're looking old. What's your name?'

Jenny Eclair, Grumpy Old Women

It's hard to be nostalgic when you can't remember anything.

Anon

Did you ever walk in a room and forget why you walked in? I think that's how dogs spend their lives.

Sue Murphy

Maturity is different from using your ailing health to blackmail your children into doing all your gardening and housework and keeping a diary for comfort and a handy reminder of what you did yesterday.

T. Kinnes

Going Gaga

Women over 50 don't have babies because they would put them down and forget where they left them.

Anon

Isn't this amazing? Clinton is getting $8 million for his memoir, Hillary got $8 million for her memoir. That is $16 million for two people who for eight years couldn't remember anything.

Jay Leno

My memory is going. I brush my teeth, and then 10 minutes later I go back and have to feel the toothbrush. Is it wet? Did I just brush them?

Terry Gilliam

I'm suffering from Mallzheimer's disease. I go to the mall and forget where I parked my car.

Anon

I think it would be interesting if old people got anti-Alzheimer's disease where they slowly began to recover other people's lost memories.

George Carlin

A Quiet Five Minutes

THE AFTERNOON NAP

I'll sleep when I'm dead.

Warren Zevon

Sleep – those little slices of death. How I loathe them.

Edgar Allan Poe

No day is so bad it can't be fixed with a nap.

Carrie Snow

Two things I dislike about my granddaughter – when she won't take her afternoon nap, and when she won't let me take mine.

Gene Perret

I usually take a two-hour nap from one to four.

Yogi Berra

A man of 60 has spent 20 years in bed and over three years in eating.

Arnold Bennett

Set aside half an hour every day to do all your worrying, then take a nap during this period.

Anon

A Quiet Five Minutes

I never take a nap after dinner but when I have had a bad night; and then the nap takes me.

Samuel Johnson

There is more refreshment and stimulation in a nap, even of the briefest, than in all the alcohol ever distilled.

Ovid

A nap, my friend, is a brief period of sleep which overtakes superannuated persons when they endeavour to entertain unwelcome visitors or to listen to scientific lectures.

George Bernard Shaw

I catnap now and then, but I think while I nap, so it's not a waste of time.

Martha Stewart

Sixty! Now is the time to make your mark on the world – explore the Antarctic or become an astronaut. Make your mind up to take on exciting new challenges – straight after your afternoon nap.

Anon

Every businessman over 50 should have a daily nap and nip; a short nap after lunch and a relaxing highball before dinner.

Dr Sara Murray Jordan

I have left orders to be awakened at any time in case of national emergency, even if I'm in a cabinet meeting.

Ronald Reagan

On the Road

DRIVING

I know it's the male menopause but I fancy a 500cc Kawasaki.

Paul Nurse

They say the first thing to go when you're old is your legs or your eyesight. It isn't true. The first thing to go is parallel parking.

Kurt Vonnegut

Mr Merton is getting on in years but he's still driving. I do worry as sometimes he forgets to indicate but he always says, 'I've lived in the same road for 40 years and I think people know where I'm going by now.'

Mrs Merton

I Stop For No Particular Reason

Car Bumper Sticker for TOGS (Terry's Old Geezers)

On the Road

What is the age people reach when they decide, when they back out of the driveway, they're not looking anymore? You know how they do that? They just go, 'Well, I'm old, and I'm backing out. I survived, let's see if you can.'

Jerry Seinfeld

When renewing my driver's licence at the age of 83 I was asked if I would like to be an organ donor. I said, 'Who would want them?'

Constance Dean

I would think the less time you have left in life, the faster you should drive. I think old people should be allowed to drive their age. If you're 80, do 80. If you're 100, do 100.

Jerry Seinfeld

Dearest Warden. Front tooth broken off; look like 81-year-old pirate, so at dentist 19a. Very old – very lame – no metras [sic].

Lady Diana Cooper, note to a traffic warden left on her car windscreen

The only reason I wear glasses is for little things, like driving my car – or finding it.

Woody Allen

On the Road

If money was no object the present I would like is a bleeper you can press as you enter the Ascot Racecourse car park to release a slow-moving firework enabling you to locate your vehicle. I very much regret the many hours I've spent in car parks around the world searching for my car.

Clement Freud

Sure, I've gotten old. I've had two bypass surgeries, a hip replacement, new knees … I've fought prostate cancer and diabetes. I'm half blind, can't hear anything quieter than a jet engine, and take 40 different medications that make me dizzy, winded and subject to blackouts. I have bouts with dementia, poor circulation, hardly feel my hands or feet any more, can't remember if I'm 85 or 92, but … thank God, I still have my Florida driver's licence.

Anon

The best car safety device is a rear-view mirror with a cop in it.

Dudley Moore

If you stay in Beverly Hills too long you become a Mercedes.

Robert Redford

Grandparents and Grandchildren

Mothers bear children. Grandmothers enjoy them.

Spanish proverb

My daughter pointed out the other day, 'A granny is only a double-decker mummy.'

Jilly Cooper

We are a grandmother.

Margaret Thatcher

I can't be a grandmother. I'm too young. Grandmothers are old. They bake and they sew. I was at Woodstock! I pissed in the fields!

Karen Buckman, Parenthood

I don't like the idea of being a 'grandmother' - old and frail and the next person to go to heaven. The result of this created image was that when I go to visit my grandchildren in Liverpool nobody offers to carry my case upstairs, and when someone's car breaks down they send for me to help push it.

Carla Lane

Grandparents and Grandchildren

Where have all the grannies gone? I mean the genuine, original, 22-carat articles who wore black shawls and cameo brooches, sat in rocking chairs and smelled of camphor?

Keith Waterhouse

True grannies were never seen in shops. They were never seen anywhere except at funerals. They did not visit their grandchildren: their grandchildren visited them. They would not have anything to do with electricity – true grannies were gas-driven.

Keith Waterhouse

Becoming a grandmother is great fun because you can use the kid to get back at your daughter.

Roseanne Barr

Grandchildren don't make me feel old. It's the knowledge that I'm married to a grandmother.

Norman Collie

Grampa Simpson: Favourite Pastimes: napping, collecting beef jerky, sending complaint letters to newspapers and politicians, going to Herman's Military Antiques Store.

The Simpsons

Grandparents and Grandchildren

Perfect love sometimes does not come till the first grandchild.

Welsh proverb

What feeling in all the world is so nice as that of a child's hand in yours? What tenderness it arouses, what power it conjures. You are instantly the very touchstone of wisdom and strength.

Marjorie Holmes

The reason grandparents and grandchildren get along so well is that they have a common enemy.

Sam Levenson

Never have children, only grandchildren.

Gore Vidal

Every generation revolts against its fathers and makes friends with its grandfathers.

Lewis Mumford

It's funny that those things your kids did that got on your nerves seem so cute when your grandchildren do them.

Raymond Holland

Does Grandpa love to babysit his grandchildren? Are you kidding? By day he is too busy taking hormone shots at the doctor's or chip shots on the golf course. At night he and Grandma are too busy doing the cha-cha.

Hal Boyle

The simplest toy, one which even the youngest child can operate, is called a grandparent.

Sam Levenson

'You're old, Nanny,' said my grandson, Tom, 'but only on the outside.'

Ellen Tate

On my 60th birthday my four-year-old grandson asked me if I was now a 'superior citizen'.

Anon

I was looking after my six-year-old grandson and I suggested we go into the garden to get some potatoes to cook for dinner. He was digging away when he suddenly looked at me with a very puzzled expression, and said, 'Nana, why do you bury your potatoes?'

Pat Boucher

My grandson was proud of his newly acquired reading skills and when I took him shopping he was reading every sign in sight. 'Look Nana,' he cried, 'Men Swear – they do, don't they?'

Angie Mayer

Grandparents and Grandchildren

My grandchildren take me to the beach and try to make words out of the veins in my legs.

Phyllis Diller

Seeing snow for the first time, my grandson jumped for joy and cried, 'Ooh, icing!'

Alex Lacey

I was reading a book to my young grandson, Adam, about a little girl who didn't know her manners. In the story, the mother gives her little girl a plate of hamburger and chips and says, 'What's the magic word?' 'Gravy!' comes the reply. 'What should she have said?' I asked. Adam didn't hesitate: 'Ketchup!'

Phyl Jarski

Playing the board-game version of *Who Wants to be a Millionaire?* with my grandchildren, a Shakespearean question came up: How many ghosts does Hamlet see? a) 1 b) 2 c) 3 d) 4. My grandson thought for a moment, then said, 'Dunno. Which play is Hamlet in?' 'Not sure,' replied my granddaughter, 'I think it was *Macbeth*.' I bought them a copy of *The Complete Works of Shakespeare* for Christmas.

Phyllis Amison

Grandparents and Grandchildren

After Sunday School, my granddaughter asked thoughtfully, 'Granddad, were you in the ark?' 'Of course not!' I replied. 'Then why weren't you drowned?'

James Potter

—Gran, you gave the baby whisky?
—Yes, it's okay. I didn't let him drive.

Jimmy Cox and Grandma, Rock Me Baby

At heart, I suspect she would like nothing better than to let go of the face-lifts and dieting and settle down to blissful grannyhood.

Julia Llewellyn Smith, on Joan Rivers

If I had known my grandchildren would be so much fun I would have had them first!

Anon

My grandfather once told me that there were two kinds of people: those who do the work and those who take the credit. He told me to try to be in the first group; there was much less competition.

Indira Gandhi

I am playing grandmothers in movies now.

Raquel Welch

Grandparents and Grandchildren

My grandmother has a bumper sticker on her car that says, 'Sexy Senior Citizen'. You don't want to think of your grandmother that way, do you: out entering wet-shawl contests? Makes you wonder where she got that dollar she gave you for your birthday.

Andy Rooney

It's amazing how grandparents seem so young once you become one.

Anon

My grandmother took a bath every year, whether she needed it or not.

Brendan Behan

Grandchildren are God's way of compensating us for growing old.

Mary H. Waldrip

An hour with your grandchildren can make you feel young again. Anything longer than that, and you start to age quickly.

Gene Perret

No cowboy was ever faster on the draw than a grandparent pulling a baby picture out of a wallet.

Anon

If God had intended us to follow recipes, He wouldn't have given us grandmothers.

Linda Henley

The best babysitters, of course, are the baby's grandparents. You feel completely comfortable entrusting your baby to them for long periods, which is why most grandparents flee to Florida.

Dave Barry

My granddaughter came to spend a few weeks with me, and I decided to teach her to sew. After I had gone through a lengthy explanation of how to thread the machine, she stepped back, put her hands on her hips, and said in disbelief, 'You mean you can do all that, but you can't play my Game Boy?'

Anon

'You're more trouble than the children are' is the greatest compliment a grandparent can receive.

Gene Perret

Grandparents Observed

My husband and I have decided to start a family while my parents are still young enough to look after them.

Rita Rudner

Grandparents Observed

My grandmother was a very tough woman. She buried three husbands. Two of them were just napping.

Rita Rudner

Grandmother, as she gets older, is not fading, but becoming more concentrated.

Paulette Alden

I was talking to my nan about Ant and Dec. She didn't know which one Dec was. I said, 'Do you know which one Ant is?' She said, 'Yes.'

Jimmy Carr

My nan has a picture of the United Kingdom tattooed over her whole body. Some people think it's weird, but you can say what you like about my nan: at least you know where you are with her.

Harry Hill

'Get Off the Gas Stove, Granny, You're Too Old to Ride the Range'

Song title

The word 'good' has many meanings. For example, if a man were to shoot his grandmother at a range of 500 yards, I should call him a good shot, but not necessarily a good man.

G.K. Chesterton

Elizabeth and Margaret coined for George V the epithet, 'Grandpa England'.

Anon

As a child, I went into the study of my grandfather, Winston Churchill. 'Grandpapa,' I said, 'is it true that you are the greatest man in the world?' 'Yes, now bugger off.'

Nicholas Soames

Market research is about as accurate as my grandmother's big toe was in predicting the weather.

Garrison Keillor

I was watching the Superbowl with my 92-year-old grandfather. The team scored a touchdown. They showed the instant replay. He thought they scored another one. I was gonna tell him, but I figured the game he was watching was better.

Steven Wright

We used to terrorize our babysitters when I was little – except for my grandfather because he used to read to us from his will.

Jan Ditullio

I'm very proud of my gold pocket watch. My grandfather, on his deathbed, sold me this watch.

Woody Allen

Grandparents Observed

My gently lachrymose grandmother had an extraordinary capacity for reliving the events of the Bible as though they were headline news in the paper.

Peter Ustinov

My grandmother was utterly convinced I'd wind up as the Archbishop of Canterbury. And, to be honest, I've never entirely ruled it out.

Hugh Grant

Helped Grandma with the weekend shopping. She was dead fierce in the grocer's; she watched the scales like a hawk watching a field mouse. Then she pounced and accused the shop assistant of giving her underweight bacon. The shop assistant was dead scared of her and put another slice on.

Sue Townsend, The Secret Diary of Adrian Mole Aged 13¾

Oh, Grannie, you shouldn't be carrying all those groceries! Next time, make two trips.

Nathan Lane

My grandma was a tall, rather stately woman, with iron-grey plaited headphones and one yellow tooth in the middle of an otherwise vacant upper set. She was in her 70s when she came to live with us and had suffered two strokes since her arrival. My brothers used to say, 'At the third stroke, she will be 70-something.'

Julie Walters, Baby Talk

Three old grannies were sitting on a park bench talking among themselves when a flasher came by. The flasher stood right in front of them, and opened his trench coat.

The first old granny had a stroke.

Then the second old granny had a stroke.

But the third old granny had arthritis and couldn't reach that far.

Anon

—Grampa kinda smells like that trunk in the garage where the bottom's all wet.

—Nuh-uh, he smells more like a photo lab.

—Stop it, both of you! Grampa smells like a regular old man, which is more like a hallway in a hospital.

Bart, Lisa and Homer Simpson, The Simpsons

Kids, your grandfather's ears are not gross. And they're certainly not an enchanted forest.

Lois Griffin, Family Guy

I loved my grandparents' home. Everything smelled older, worn but safe; the food aroma had baked itself into the furniture.

Susan Strasberg

My Hungarian grandfather was the kind of man that could follow someone into a revolving door and come out first.

Stephen Fry

There's one thing about children: they never go around showing snapshots of their grandparents.

Bessie & Beulah

Golfing Grandpas

If you watch a game, it's fun. If you play it, it's recreation. If you work at it, it's golf.

Bob Hope

Golf is a good walk spoiled.

Mark Twain

Golf is more fun than walking naked in a strange place, but not much.

Buddy Hackett

Playing golf is like going to a strip joint. After 18 holes you're tired and most of your balls are missing.

Tim Allen

Golfing Grandpas

The uglier a man's legs are, the better he plays golf – it's almost a law.

H. G. Wells

Golf is a fascinating game. It has taken me nearly 40 years to discover that I can't play it.

Ted Ray

When I die, bury me on the golf course so my husband will visit.

Anon

I would like to deny all allegations by Bob Hope that during my last game of golf, I hit an eagle, a birdie, an elk and a moose.

Gerald Ford

I'll shoot my age if I have to live to be 105.

Bob Hope

The only time my prayers are never answered is on the golf course.

Billy Graham

Sex and golf are the two things you can enjoy even if you're not good at them.

Kevin Costner

Golfing Grandpas

I know I'm getting better at golf because I'm hitting fewer spectators.

Gerald Ford

Eric: My wife says if I don't give up golf, she'll leave me.
Ernie: That's terrible.
Eric: I know – I'm really going to miss her.

Eric Morecombe and Ernie Wise

It was cool for a couple of weeks, but how much bad golf can you play?

John Goodman

It took me 17 years to get 3,000 hits in baseball. I did it in one afternoon on the golf course.

Hank Aaron

I had a wonderful experience on the golf course today. I had a hole in nothing. Missed the ball and sank the divot.

Don Adams

In the Bob Hope Golf Classic, the participation of President Gerald Ford was more than enough to remind you that the nuclear button was at one stage at the disposal of a man who might have either pressed it by mistake or else pressed it deliberately in order to obtain room service.

Clive James

The only way to enjoy golf is to be a masochist. Go out and beat yourself to death.

Howard Keel

If you think it's hard to meet new people, try picking up the wrong golf ball.

Jack Lemmon

If I wasn't an actor I'd be unemployable, or at best the secretary to a golf club somewhere. Nine holes at that, and blue in the face with port.

David Niven

I can't hit a ball more than 200 yards. I have no butt. You need a butt if you're going to hit a golf ball.

Dennis Quaid

I'm patient with crossword puzzles and the most impatient golfer.

Brett Hull

Golf is a day spent in a round of strenuous idleness.

William Wordsworth

Golfing Grandpas

I would rather play *Hamlet* with no rehearsal than TV golf.

Jack Lemmon

If you are caught on a golf course during a storm and are afraid of lightning, hold up a 1-iron. Not even God can hit a 1-iron.

Lee Trevino

Sport is a wonderful metaphor for life. Of all the sports that I played – skiing, baseball, fishing – there is no greater example than golf, because you're playing against yourself and nature.

Robert Redford

I don't have a life, I really don't. I'm as close to a nun as you can be without the little hat. I'm a golf nun.

Gabrielle Reece

In my retirement I go for a short swim at least once or twice every day. It's either that or buy a new golf ball.

Gene Perret

The reason the pro tells you to keep your head down is so you can't see him laughing.

Phyllis Diller

If you drink, don't drive. Don't even putt.

Dean Martin

If you are going to throw a club, it is important to throw it ahead of you, down the fairway, so you don't have to waste energy going back to pick it up.

Tommy Bolt

Acting has been good to me. It's taken me to play golf all over the world.

Christopher Lee

It is almost impossible to remember how tragic a place the world is when one is playing golf.

Robert Lynd

Long ago, when men cursed and beat the ground with sticks, it was called witchcraft. Today, it's called golf.

Anon

Golf: a game where white men can dress up as black pimps and get away with it.

Robin Williams

The golf course is the only place I can go dressed like a pimp and fit in perfectly. Anywhere else, lime-green pants and alligator shoes, I got a cop on my ass.

Samuel L. Jackson

I'm a coloured, one-eyed Jew… do I need anything else?

Sammy Davis Jr., in answer to a question: What's your golf handicap?

The place of the father in the modern suburban family is a very small one, particularly if he plays golf.

Bertrand Russell

Everyone's Favourite Grandmother

QUEEN ELIZABETH, THE QUEEN MOTHER (1900–2002)

The Queen Mother seemed incapable of a bad performance as a national grandmother – warm, smiling, human, understanding, she embodied everything the public could want of its grandmother.

John Pearson

—I'm going to live to be 100.
—Then it will be Charles who'll send you your centenarian telegram.

The Queen Mother and Queen Elizabeth II

I've got to go and see the old folk.

The Queen Mother, 97, spotting a group of pensioners at Cheltenham Racecourse

Is it me or are pensioners getting younger these days?

The Queen Mother, 100, presenting prizes at an old people's garden competition

Horse racing is one of the real sports that's left to us: a bit of danger and excitement, and the horses, which are the best thing in the world.

The Queen Mother

I keep a thermos flask full of Champagne. It's one of my little treats.

The Queen Mother

There is all the difference in the world between the patient's meaning of the word 'comfortable' and the surgeon's.

The Queen Mother after she was described as 'comfortable' following an operation

Choppers have changed my life as conclusively as that of Anne Boleyn.

The Queen Mother on helicopters

Everyone's Favourite Grandmother

When one is 18, one has very definite dislikes, but as one grows older, one becomes more tolerant, and finds that nearly everyone is, in some degree, nice.

The Queen Mother

She is a law unto herself and takes no notice of advice.

Aide to the Queen Mother

A glass of wine with lunch? Is that wise? You know you have to reign all afternoon.

The Queen Mother to Queen Elizabeth II

—Who do you think you are?
—Mummy, the Queen.

The Queen Mother and Queen Elizabeth II

For goodness' sake, don't let Mummy have another drink.

Queen Elizabeth II to a page-boy

Don't retouch my wrinkles in the photograph. I would not want it to be thought that I had lived for all these years without having anything to show for it.

The Queen Mother

I love life – that's my secret.

The Queen Mother

Hers was a great old age, but not a cramped one. She remained young at heart, and the young themselves sensed that.

Dr George Carey, Archbishop of Canterbury

She seemed gloriously unstoppable and ever since I was a child I adored her. Her houses were always filled with an atmosphere of fun, laughter and affection.

Prince Charles

Anything that was meant to be formal and went wrong, she enjoyed. She laughed herself stupid about it. It kept us all sane. She loved to hear about my friends and all they got up to. And she loved to hear about how much trouble I got into at school.

Prince William

She saw the funny side of life and we laughed till we cried. Oh, how I shall miss those laughs and the wonderful wisdom born of so much experience and of an innate sensitivity to life.

Prince Charles

My favourite photograph of us together is a picture of me aged about 9 or 10 helping the Queen Mother up the steps of Windsor Castle. I remember the moment because she said to me: 'Keep doing that for people and you will go a long way in life.'

Prince William

—One Christmas, we were sitting watching Ali G on TV. We were laughing when my great-grandmother came in. She saw Ali G click his fingers and say 'Respec', and Harry and I showed her what to do. After three goes she had it. Later that day, when we were all having Christmas lunch, she tried it out.
—It was the end of the meal, and she stood up and said, 'Darling, lunch was marvellous – respec',' and clicked her fingers. Everyone burst out laughing.

Prince William and Prince Harry

Before I went to St Andrew's, she gave me a farewell lunch. As she said goodbye, she said, 'Any good parties, invite me down.' But there was no way. I knew full well that if I invited her down, she would dance me under the table.

Prince William

She was, quite simply, the most magical grandmother you could possibly have.

Prince Charles

Parents and Children

Avenge yourself. Live long enough to be a problem to your children.

Kirk Douglas

All right, since your parents are coming, I did the standard pre-parent sweep. Which means if you're looking for your 'neck massager' it's under the bed.

Jimmy Cox, Rock Me Baby

—Homer, are you really going to ignore your father for the rest of your life?
—Of course not, Marge, just for the rest of his life.

Marge and Homer Simpson, The Simpsons

You might notice your ageing parents have both become abnormally attached to some kind of pet, a dog or a cat that they got after all the kids left home. They buy it sweaters and birthday gifts and they have conversations with it that are often longer and more meaningful than the ones they have with you.

Dave Barry

—Dorothy, why don't we bond?
—Mom, we're from before bonding and quality time.

Dorothy Zbornak and Sophia Petrillo, The Golden Girls

Stay another bloody week? Over my dead body! She makes me un-bloody-plug everything at night before we go to bed – but she's got herself a bloody electric blanket on all night.

Jim Royle, The Royle Family

Parents and Children

—You must miss Prince Andrew, Ma'am, when he's away in the Navy?
—Indeed I do. Especially because he is the only one in the family who knows how to work the video.

Visitor and Queen Elizabeth II

My parents did a really scary thing recently. They bought a caravan. This means that they can pull up in front of my house anytime now and just live there.

Paula Poundstone

My parents live in a retirement community, which is basically a minimum-security prison with a golf course.

Joel Warshaw

Why do so many old people live in those minimum-security prisons? What's with all the security? Are the old people trying to escape, or are people stealing old people?

Jerry Seinfeld

Knowing as I do Frasier's relationship with his father, when he informed me he had taken him in to live with him, I immediately flipped to the weather channel to see if hell had indeed frozen over.

Lilith Sternen, Frasier

—It seems like only yesterday that Dad moved in with you.
—Isn't it interesting that two people can have completely opposite impressions of the same event?

Niles and Frasier Crane, Frasier

—Onslow, Father's on the roof again!
—Ask him if he's got my bottle opener!

Rose and Onslow, Keeping Up Appearances

From the vantage point of his wondrously serene old age, my father contemplates our lives almost as if they were books he can dip into whenever he wants. His back pages, perhaps.

Angela Carter

As you get older, your dad gets smaller. When I went home last time, he'd practically disappeared.

Jeff Green

My father has lived so long that everything is forgiven, even his habit of referring to the present incumbent by my first husband's name.

Angela Carter

No matter how old a mother is, she watches her middle-aged children for signs of improvement.

Florida Scott-Maxwell

Parents and Children

I am 102 years of age. I have no worries since my youngest son went into an old folk's home.

Victoria Bedwell

Children are a great comfort in your old age. They help you reach it faster, too.

Lionel Kauffman

My parents just arrived back from Singapore on the *QE2* and invited me for dinner on board the ship. 'So,' my father said, leaning back in the antique chair with a smug expression, 'enjoying your inheritance? I know I am.' He and my mother couldn't stop laughing.

Chris McEvoy

Your kids will forgive you someday. Of course, by then you'll be dead.

Sophia Petrillo, The Golden Girls

Always be nice to your children, because they are the ones who will choose your rest home.

Phyllis Diller

Twilight Homes for the Bewildered

Retirement homes are great. It's like being a baby, only you're old enough to appreciate it.

Homer Simpson, The Simpsons

The colour brochure for the Dunraven Sunset Facility showed artists' impressions of cleanly dressed oldsters watching TV and Zimmering around in rose gardens, smiling like those people you see on the Air Safety card as they slither down emergency chutes or calmly inflate each other's whistles.

Dame Edna Everage

I've got a placement as a volunteer at an old folk's day centre. They've got this 'companion scheme' where we chat informatively to the old-timers about the issues of the day, and in return they sort of tell us stories about rationing and how chicken used to taste like chicken.

Tony, Men Behaving Badly

Nursing homes. Ugh. I hate those places. All the old people want to touch my hair.

Claire Fisher, Six Feet Under

I could smell the funny odour rest homes always seem to have: a mixture of roast lamb, chloroform and little jobs.

Dame Edna Everage

My mother's suffering from advanced old-timer's disease so we've put her in a maximum-security Twilight Home for the Bewildered. Her accommodation is in the Sylvia Plath Suite. Other wards include the Virginia Woolf Incontinence Wing, the Diane Arbus X-ray Unit, and the Zelda Fitzgerald Fire Escape.

Dame Edna Everage

Spicing up the Twilight Years

Once the travel bug bites there is no known antidote, and I know that I shall be happily infected until the end of my life.

Michael Palin

Football and cookery are the two most important subjects in this country.

Delia Smith

Life may not be the party we hoped for, but while we are here we might as well dance.

J. Williams

Give a man a fish and he has food for a day. Teach him how to fish and you can get rid of him for the entire weekend.

Zenna Schaffer

One of the worst things that can happen in life is to win a bet on a horse at an early age.

Danny McGoorty, Irish pool player

If people concentrated on the really important things in life, there'd be a shortage of fishing poles.

Doug Larson

There is a very fine line between 'hobby' and 'mental illness'.

Dave Barry

Hell, if I'd jumped on all the dames I'm supposed to have jumped on, I'd have had no time to go fishing.

Clark Gable

I go to Alaska and fish salmon. I do some halibut fishing, lake fishing, trout fishing, fly fishing. I look quite good in waders. I love my waders. I don't think there is anything sexier than just standing in waders with a fly rod. I just love it.

Linda Hamilton

I only make movies to finance my fishing.

Lee Marvin

Fishing is boring, unless you catch an actual fish, and then it is disgusting.

Dave Barry

I'm always suspicious of games where you're the only ones that play it.

Jack Charlton, on hurling

Skiing consists of wearing $3,000 worth of clothes and equipment and driving 200 miles in the snow in order to stand around at a bar and drink.

P.J. O'Rourke

There's a fine line between fishing and just standing on the shore like an idiot.

Steven Wright

Skiing combines outdoor fun with knocking down trees with your face.

Dave Barry

My First 100 Years

On 14 January, Rose will be 100 years old, and she's looking forward to receiving a telegram from the Queen. It seems a scant reward for what is, after all, a century. Come on Queen Elizabeth, give us some incentive!

Mrs Merton

I don't want to live to be 100. I don't think I could stand to see bell-bottom trousers three times.

Jeff Foxworthy

Who wants to live to be 100? Anyone who's 99.

Billy Wilder

If you live to be 100, I want to live to be 100 minus one day, so I never have to live without you.

Winnie the Pooh

Turning 100 was the worst birthday of my life. I wouldn't wish it on my worst enemy. Turning 101 was not so bad. Once you're past that century mark, it's just not shocking.

Bessie Delany

If I'd known I was gonna live this long, I'd have taken better care of myself.

Eubie Blake, 100

Research shows that centenarians are the healthiest group of people in the world. How do you think they got to be 100 years old? Because they don't get sick.

John Stark

Yes I'm 100. I put it down to 30 years of safe sex and boneless fish.

Annie Miller

You can live to be 100 by giving up all the things that make you want to live to be 100.

Woody Allen

A centenarian is a person who has lived to be 100 years of age. He never smoked or he smoked all his life. He never drank whiskey or he drank whiskey for 80 years. He was a vegetarian or he wasn't a vegetarian. Follow these rules closely and you, too, can become a centenarian.

Stephen Leacock

One thing that unites all centenarians is that they have wonderful senses of humour. They use it for all kinds of things, like joking about death. The thought of dying is no big deal; they've had time to prepare.

Margery Silver

I have been asked to pose for *Penthouse* on my 100th birthday. Everybody is going to be sorry.

Dolly Parton

Secrets of Long Life

—To what do you attribute your long life?
—To the fact that I haven't died yet.

Sir Malcolm Sargent

To what do I attribute my longevity? Bad luck, mostly.

Billy Wilder

My father died at 102. Whenever I would ask what kept him going, he'd answer, 'I never worry.'

Jerry Stiller

—Happy 103rd Birthday, Mr Zukor. What is the secret of your long life?
—I gave up smoking two years ago.

Adolph Zukor

Secrets of Long Life

Good Things About Being the Oldest Person in the World: You make *The Guinness Book of Records* without doing a damn thing; at your 100th-year high-school reunion, you've got the buffet all to yourself; you don't need denture cleaner – you can just call the grandchildren and borrow theirs; you can suck at golf and still shoot your age; you can smoke all you damn well please.

David Letterman

Bad Things About Being the Oldest Person in the World: seems like every time you turn around that damn Halley's Comet is back; shoulder-length ear hair; you get to see your great-great-great-grandchildren marry moon men; all the shoes.

David Letterman

It's a proven fact: gardeners live longer. You are young at any age if you are planning for tomorrow and gardeners are always looking forward, anticipating new shoots.

Mira Nair

You live longer once you realize that any time spent being unhappy is wasted.

Ruth E. Renkl

Women don't live longer. It just seems longer.

Erma Bombeck

Scientists say that women who have children after 40 are more likely to live to be 100, but they don't know why. I think the reason is, they're waiting for the day when their kids move out of the house.

Lorrie Moss

—What is your prescription for a healthy long life?
—Never deny yourself anything.

Mr Justice Holmes

Ciggie-loving Marie Ellis was laid to rest yesterday – after living to 105 despite smoking nearly half a million fags. She was cremated clutching a packet of her favourite Benson & Hedges. Staff and residents from the nursing home sent her off with a chorus of 'Smoke Gets In Your Eyes'.

Sun *newspaper*

Alcohol is good for you. My grandfather proved it irrevocably. He drank two quarts of booze every mature day of his life and lived to the age of 103. I was at the cremation – the fire would not go out.

Dave Astor

I can only assume that it is largely due to the accumulation of toasts to my health over the years that I am still enjoying a fairly satisfactory state of health and have reached such an unexpectedly great age.

The Duke of Edinburgh, 80

Secrets of Long Life

My three rules for a long life are regular exercise, hobbies and complete avoidance of midget gems.

Kitty, Victoria Wood

I credit my youthfulness at 80 to the fact of a cheerful disposition and contentment in every period of my life with what I was.

Oliver Wendell Holmes

At 70, I'm in fine fettle for my age, sleep like a babe and feel around 12. The secret? Lots of meat, drink and cigarettes and not giving in to things.

Jennifer Paterson

The secret of my long life? Swim, dance a little, go to Paris every August, and live within walking distance of two hospitals.

Dr Horatio Luro

My grandmother just passed away; she was 104 years old. I went to buy some flowers and the guy there says, 'Ooh, 104? How'd she die?' How'd she die? She was 104! I told him, 'Well, it's alright – they saved the baby.'

Larry the Cable Guy

Secrets of Long Life

I attribute my long and healthy life to the fact that I never touched a cigarette, a drink, or a girl until I was 10 years old.

George Moore

—What is the secret of your long life?
—Keep breathing.

Sophie Tucker

If you want a long life, several years before birth, advertise for a couple of parents belonging to long-lived families.

Oliver Wendell Holmes

No one's so old that he doesn't think he could hope for one more day.

Seneca

If you survive long enough, you're revered – rather like an old building.

Katharine Hepburn

If you live to be 90 in England and can still eat a boiled egg, they think you deserve the Nobel Prize.

Alan Bennett

A Grand Old Man is anyone with snow-white hair who has kept out of jail till 80.

Stephen Leacock

I've never known a person who lives to 110 who is remarkable for anything else.

Josh Billings

Great men, men who change the world, don't usually die of old age. Somebody kills them. Think of Jesus, Martin Luther King Jr, JFK.

D.H. Hughley

—You've reached the ripe old age of 121. What do you expect the future will be like?
—Very short.

Interviewer and Jeanne Calment (1875–1997)

I'm Gonna Live Forever

If man were immortal, do you realise what his meat bills would be?

Woody Allen

To lengthen thy life, lessen thy meals.

Benjamin Franklin

I'm Gonna Live Forever

The secret to a long life is to stay busy, get plenty of exercise, and don't drink too much. Then again, don't drink too little.

Hermann Smith-Johansson, at age 103

Pretend to be dumb: that's the only way to reach old age.

Friedrich Dürrenmatt

A man 90 years old was asked to what he attributed his longevity.

'I reckon,' he said, with a twinkle in his eye, 'it's because most nights I went to bed and slept when I should have sat up and worried.'

Dorothea Kent

If you live to the age of a hundred you've made it because very few people die past the age of a hundred.

George Burns

My formula for living is quite simple. I get up in the morning and I go to bed at night. In between, I occupy myself as best I can.

Cary Grant

The only real way to look younger is not to be born so soon.

Charles M. Schulz

I'm Gonna Live Forever

I've already lived about 20 years longer than my life expectancy at the time I was born. That's a source of annoyance to a great many people.

Ronald Reagan

I wanna live till I die: no more, no less.

Eddie Izzard

He had decided to live forever or die in the attempt.

Joseph Heller

Ageing seems to be the only available way to live a long life.

Daniel Auber

Roz: Physical contact extends our lives.
Frasier: Well then, you'll outlive Styrofoam.

Frasier

I postpone death by living, by suffering, by error, by risking, by giving, by losing.

Anaïs Nin

I am long on ideas, but short on time. I expect to live to be only about a hundred.

Thomas Alva Edison

I'm Gonna Live Forever

We could certainly slow the ageing process down if it had to work its way through Congress.

Anon

My secret for staying young is good food, plenty of rest, and a make-up man with a spray-gun.

Bob Hope

I'd like to grow very old as slowly as possible.

Irene Mayer Selznick

My only fear is that I may live too long. This would be a subject of dread to me.

Thomas Jefferson

I would not live forever, because we should not live forever, because if we were supposed to live forever, then we would live forever, but we cannot live forever, which is why I would not live forever.

Miss Alabama, 1994 Miss USA contest

Porridge is also the secret to a long life. I have it in the morning and it's the best start to the day.

Anon

The Oldest Swinger in Town

LOVE AND COURTSHIP

Your place, or back to the sheltered accommodation?

Barry Cryer

Hi, I'm Marv, your grandmother's gentleman-caller, or as you kids would say, her booty call.

Marv, Rock Me Baby

'When My Love Comes Back from the Ladies' Room Will I Be Too Old to Care?'

Lewis Grizzard, song title

They say a man is as old as the woman he feels. In that case, I'm 85.

Groucho Marx

Only flirt with women who flirt with you or you can end up looking like those old rich gents in night-clubs, proudly photographed with their arms round bimbos whose interest was clearly in the old geezer's bank balance rather than in his wrinkled and lined person.

George Melly

Hugh Hefner now has several girlfriends – one for each day of the week. Someone needs to tell him that those are nurses.

Jay Leno

When we were young, you made me blush,
go hot and cold, and turn to mush.
I still feel all these things, it's true –
but is it menopause, or you?

Susan Anderson

As you get older, the pickings get slimmer, but the people don't.

Carrie Fisher

Gentleman, retired, knocking on a bit. Own teeth and hair. Seeks lady (45 plus) for raw sex.

Lonely hearts ad

Before I turn 67, I would like to have a lot of sex with a man I like. If you want to talk first, Trollope works for me.

Jane Juska, personal ad, The New York Times Review of Books

The Oldest Swinger in Town

I was introduced to a beautiful young lady as a gentleman in his 90s. Early 90s, I insisted.

George Burns

Delighted you came, my dear, and I'd like you to know that you made a happy man feel very old.

Terry-Thomas, The Last Remake of Beau Geste

—You wrote in a story that when you reached the age of 84 you would commit suicide. Why have you not done so?
—Laziness and cowardice prevent me. Besides, I am constantly falling in love.

Jorge Luis Borges

It's never too late to have a fling
For Autumn is just as nice as Spring
And it's never too late to fall in love.

Sandy Wilson

Nothing makes people crosser than being considered too old for love.

Nancy Mitford

I have almost done with harridans, and shall soon become old enough to fall in love with girls of 14.

Jonathan Swift

The Oldest Swinger in Town

When one is 20, yes, but at 47, Venus may rise from the sea, and I for one should hardly put on my spectacles to have a look.

William Thackeray

Trouble is, by the time you can read a girl like a book, your library card has expired.

Milton Berle

Age does not protect you from love. But love, to some extent, protects you from age.

Jeanne Moreau

Those who love deeply never grow old; they may die of old age, but they die young.

Benjamin Franklin

The lovely thing about being 40 is that you can appreciate 25-year-old men more.

Colleen McCullough

There ain't nothin' an ol' man can do but bring me a message from a young one.

'Moms' Mabley

I think older women with younger men threaten all the right people.

William Hamilton

The Oldest Swinger in Town

The advantages of dating younger men is that on them everything, like hair and teeth, is in the right place as opposed to being on the bedside table or bathroom floor.

Candace Bushnell

I don't date women my own age. There aren't any.

Milton Berle

The older woman's love is not love of herself, nor of herself mirrored in a lover's eyes, nor is it corrupted by need. It is a feeling of tenderness so still and deep and warm that it gilds every grass blade and blesses every fly. I wouldn't have missed it for the world.

Germaine Greer

I thought nobody would touch me again – not until the undertaker.

May, The Mother

—I do love the rain so. It reminds me of my first kiss.
—Ah, your first kiss was in the rain?
—No, it was in the shower.

Blanche Devereaux and Dorothy Zbornak, The Golden Girls

Learning to love yourself is the greatest love of all, says George Benson in the popular song. I learned to love myself in the early 1980s and have never looked back.

Mrs Merton

Marriage

When marrying, ask yourself this question: do you believe that you will be able to converse well with this person into your old age? Everything else in marriage is transitory.

Friedrich Nietzsche

It's quite a romantic idea, growing old together. Sitting on park benches, feeding the ducks, leafing gently through *Saga* magazine.

Dorothy, Men Behaving Badly

Walking down the aisle together after they'd just married, Michael Denison turned to his new wife, Dulcie Gray, and whispered, 'Just think, darling, only 50 years off our golden wedding anniversary!' He died just before they reached their 60th anniversary.

Alan Marks

Marriage

I want to be married to my wife until we forget each other's names. My wife is the only one who knows what I used to be; and she is starting to lose a little of it, too, so we are breaking down in tandem.

Bill Cosby

An archaeologist is the best husband a woman can have; the older she gets, the more interested he is in her.

Agatha Christie

Whatever you may look like, marry a man your own age – as your beauty fades, so will his eyesight.

Phyllis Diller

Carol Channing, 82, star of the hit musical, *Hello, Dolly!*, wrote fondly about her high school sweetheart, Harry Kullijian, in her memoir, *Just Lucky*. Kullijian, 83, read the book, got in touch with Carol, and now they've got married. 'He's exactly the same now as he was when we were 12,' said Ms Channing.

Amy Robinson

We've managed 24 years of marriage – with a lot of broken crockery along the way.

Eileen Atkins

My wife and I have just celebrated our 30th wedding anniversary. If I had killed her the first time I thought about it, I'd be out of prison by now.

Frank Carson

My parents have a very good marriage. They've been together forever. They've passed their silver and gold anniversaries. The next one is rust.

Rita Rudner

I gave him the best years of my thighs.

Dorothy Zbornak, The Golden Girls

My parents stayed together for 40 years but that was out of spite.

Woody Allen

I've been married so long I'm on my third bottle of Tabasco.

Susan Vass

The best way to get a husband to do anything is to suggest that he is too old to do it.

Felicity Parker

Marriage

When you live with another person for 50 years, all your memories are invested in that person, like a bank account of shared memories. Thus, the past is part of the present as long as the other person lives. It is better than any scrapbook, because you are both living scrapbooks.

Federico Fellini

Love is what you've been through with somebody.

James Thurber

My notion of a wife at 40 is that a man should be able to change her, like a bank note, for two 20s.

Douglas Jerrold

I wouldn't be caught dead marrying a woman old enough to be my wife.

Tony Curtis

When a man of 60 runs off with a young woman, I'm never surprised. I have a sneaking admiration for him. After all, he's going to need it.

Deborah Kerr

He has a future and I have a past, so we should be all right.

Jennie Churchill, 64, marrying Montagu Porch, 41

When people ask me, *sotto voce* in surprise, 'So what about the age difference between you and your husband, Percy?' I usually shrug, smile and quip, 'So, if he dies, he dies.'

Joan Collins

You're too old to get married again. Not only can't you cut the mustard, honey, you're too old to open the jar.

Bob Hope

I was once engaged when I was 40, and I found it gave me very serious constipation. So I broke off the engagement and the lady quite understood.

Fellow of Trinity College, Cambridge, 97

Being an old maid is like death by drowning – a really delightful sensation after you have ceased struggling.

Edna Ferber

My wife and I were happy for 20 years. Then we met.

Rodney Dangerfield

I married the first man I ever kissed. When I tell this to my children they just about throw up.

Barbara Bush

Marriage

Some people ask the secret of our long marriage. We take time to go to a restaurant two times a week. A little candlelight, dinner, soft music and dancing. She goes Tuesdays, I go Fridays.

Henny Youngman

My wife and I tried to breakfast together, but we had to stop or our marriage would have been wrecked.

Winston Churchill

In mid-life the man wants to see how irresistible he still is to younger women. How they turn their hearts to stone and more or less commit a murder of their marriage I just don't know, but they do.

Patricia Neal

When asked his secret of love, being married 54 years to the same person, he said, 'Ruth and I are happily incompatible.'

Billy Graham

I've been in love with the same woman for 49 years. If my wife ever finds out, she'll kill me.

Henny Youngman

Ann Meara of the comedy team Stiller and Meara observed a while ago in a *New York Times* interview of her 30-plus-year marriage, 'Was it love at first sight? It wasn't then – but it sure is now.'

Ann Meara

You, that are going to be married, think things can never be done too fast: but we that are old, and know what we are about, must elope methodically, madam.

Oliver Goldsmith

No man or woman really knows what perfect love is until they have been married a quarter of a century.

Mark Twain

My new wife is 32 and I'm 70. She's rejuvenated me totally. It's so exciting to see life through the eyes of a modern girl.

Wilbur Smith

Sheila and I just celebrated our 30th wedding anniversary. Somebody asked her what was our secret. She answered, 'On my wedding day, I decided to make a list of 10 of Tim's faults which, for the sake of our marriage, I would always overlook. I figured I could live with at least 10!' When she was asked which faults she had listed, Sheila replied, 'I never did get around to listing them. Instead, every time he does something that makes me mad, I simply say to myself, "Lucky for him, it's one of the 10!"'

Tim Hudson, Chicken Soup for the Romantic Soul

Marriage

There is no greater happiness for a man than approaching a door at the end of a day knowing someone on the other side of that door is waiting for the sound of his footsteps.

Ronald Reagan

The other night I said to my wife, Ruth, 'Do you feel that the sex and excitement have gone out of our marriage?' She said, 'I'll discuss it with you during the next commercial.'

Milton Berle

One Christmas my husband gave me a chenille hand-knitted bobble hat. It was like we'd never met. I opened it and I said, 'Did you not like me when you bought me this?'

Arabella Weir

I'd marry again if I found a man who had 15 million dollars, would sign over half to me, and guarantee that he'd be dead within a year.

Bette Davis

I've had an exciting time. I married for love and got a little money along with it.

Rose Fitzgerald Kennedy

We were just happy to be in the same room together.

Judi Dench, on her long marriage to Michael Williams

Before marriage, a man will lie awake all night thinking about something you've said. After marriage, he'll fall asleep before you finish saying it.

Helen Rowland

I suppose when they reach a certain age some men are afraid to grow up. It seems the older the men get, the younger their new wives get.

Elizabeth Taylor

As you get older, you realise it's work. It's that fine line between love and companionship. But passionate love? I'd love to know how to make that last.

Tracey Ullman

All marriages are happy. It's trying to live together afterwards that causes all the problems.

Shelley Winters

Instead of getting married again, I'm going to find a woman I don't like and just give her a house.

Rod Stewart

Marriage

The man or woman you really love will never grow old to you. Through the wrinkles of time, through the bowed frame of years, you will always see the dear face and feel the warm heart union of your eternal love.

Alfred A. Montapert

My husband, like most men, can only do one thing at a time. If there's two cups of tea to be made, they'll make one. And then they'll make another one after that. If my husband's going to the shop and I say, 'Can you get a loaf of bread and a pint of milk?' he'll come back with one or the other. Never both.

Linda Robson, Grumpy Old Women

Before marriage, a man will lay down his life for you; after marriage he won't even lay down his newspaper.

Helen Rowland

Marriage is like a cage; one sees the birds outside desperate to get in, and those inside desperate to get out.

Ogden Nash

The conception of two people living together for 25 years without having a cross word suggests a lack of spirit only to be admired in sheep.

Alan Patrick Herber

My wife Mary and I have been married for 47 years and not once have we had an argument serious enough to consider divorce; murder, yes, but divorce, never.

Jack Benny

Men have got no reason to be grumpy at all [at Christmas time], because they don't have to do anything. They really don't do anything. In fact, my husband goes out on Christmas Eve to buy my present. He's had 364 days to go and get it, and he goes on Christmas Eve.

Linda Robson, Grumpy Old Women

I never knew what real happiness was until I got married, and by then it was too late.

Max Kaufman

Bigamy is having one wife too many. Marriage is the same.

Oscar Wilde

That married couples can live together day after day is a miracle that the Vatican has overlooked.

Bill Cosby

After about 20 years of marriage, I'm finally starting to scratch the surface of that one. And I think the answer lies somewhere between conversation and chocolate.

Mel Gibson, when asked if he knew what women want

Marriage

We do not squabble, fight or have rows. We collect grudges. We're in an arms race, storing up warheads for the domestic Armageddon.

Hugh Leonard

On my 60th birthday my wife gave me a superb birthday present. She let me win an argument.

Anon

Basically my wife was immature. I'd be at home in the bath and she'd come in and sink my boats.

Woody Allen

Women! I have no idea. I don't know anything about women at all. They're a complete mystery to me.

Bryan Ferry

I was married for 30 years. Isn't that enough? I've had my share of dirty underwear on the floor.

Martha Stewart

Your marriage is in trouble if your wife says, 'You're only interested in one thing,' and you can't remember what it is.

Milton Berle

There's one thing about a late marriage – it doesn't last long.

Elderly Irishman, talking on Irish TV about courting in the 1940s

A friend recently told us about a 25th anniversary party where the husband gave a toast and said, 'The key to our success is very simple. Within minutes after every fight, one of us says, "I'm sorry, Sally".'

Cokie and Steve Roberts

I haven't spoken to my wife in years. I didn't want to interrupt her.

Rodney Dangerfield

We are so fond of one another, because our ailments are the same.

Jonathan Swift

To see a young couple loving each other is no wonder, but to see an old couple loving each other is the best sight of all.

William Makepeace Thackeray

I swear there are drugs in the upholstery of his chair. Because honestly he just gets near the television and goes 'Zzz...' It's known as the drugged chair.

Dillie Keane, Grumpy Old Women

Sex

A little old lady in the nursing home holds up her clenched fist and announces, 'Anyone who can guess what I have in my closed hand can have sex with me tonight.' An elderly gentleman calls out, 'An elephant.' 'Close enough,' she replies.

Anon

When the grandmothers of today hear the word 'Chippendales', they don't necessarily think of chairs.

Jean Kerr

I haven't yet reached the stage where I'd agree that liniment oil is a decent replacement for sex.

Stephanie Beacham

It's ill-becoming for an old broad to sing about how bad she wants it. But occasionally we do.

Lena Horne

—There's a man on our lawn.
—Get a net!

Dorothy Zbornak and Blanche Devereaux, The Golden Girls

Let's do it! Let's do it! I really want to rant and rave.
Let's go, 'cause I know, just how I want you to behave:
Not bleakly. Not meekly.
Beat me on the bottom with a *Woman's Weekly*.
Let's do it! Let's do it! Let's do it tonight!

Victoria Wood

Pass me my teeth, and I'll bite you.

George Burns

An old broom knows the dirty corners best.

Irish proverb

My mother-in-law was on holiday in Italy with friends in a villa situated at the end of an unlit, perilous path. A torch was found to light the way but it had no batteries. 'I know,' said my mother-in-law's friend, a lady in her early 60s, 'I'll use the ones out of my vibrator.'

Janice Turner

Of all the faculties, the last to leave us is sexual desire. That means that long after wearing bifocals and hearing aids, we'll still be making love. We just won't know with whom.

Jack Paar

Sex

If you cannot catch a bird of paradise, better take a wet hen.

Russian proverb

The great thing about sex when you're older is that you don't have to worry about getting pregnant.

Barbra Streisand

I can still enjoy sex at 75. I live at 76, so it's no distance.

Bob Monkhouse

There's a lot of promiscuity about these days, and I'm all for it.

Ben Travers, 94

In the theatre I'm playing, there's a hole in the wall between the ladies' dressing room and mine. I've been meaning to plug it up, but what the hell … let 'em enjoy themselves.

George Burns, 82

On my 85th birthday, I felt like a 20-year-old. But there wasn't one around.

Milton Berle

I prefer young girls. Their stories are shorter.

Thomas McGuane

At my age I like threesomes – in case one of us dies.

Rodney Dangerfield

I think that Viagra and the Pill are the two most important inventions of the second half of the 20th century.

Hugh Hefner

Now that I'm 78, I do tantric sex because it's very slow. My favourite position is called the plumber. You stay in all day but nobody comes.

John Mortimer

I'm 78 but I still use a condom when I have sex. I can't take the damp.

Alan Gregory

Just because you're in your 70s doesn't mean you can't still swing. All the old geezers throw their false teeth onto the table, the ladies pick a set and hook up with the owner.

Anon

People are startled by my books because they think, how can an old woman write about sex? The idea that people go on being sexy all their life is little explored in fiction. What do people think 'happy ever after' means? It goes on and on; it doesn't end.

Mary Wesley

Sex

As I grow older and older and totter towards the tomb, I find that I care less and less who goes to bed with whom.

Dorothy L. Sayers

I'm at the stage of life when I'd give up a night of wild rapture with Denzel Washington for a nice report on my next bone-density test.

Judith Viorst

In my mid-60s, what I find the hardest to bear is being 'safe'. After a gym session I found myself in the Jacuzzi with a gorgeous young brunette. We had a wonderful chat, laughing and joking. But it was awful. Sitting there in her skimpy bikini, she did not see me as even slightly dangerous.

Peter Church

I have no sex appeal. A Peeping Tom saw me and pulled down the shade.

Phyllis Diller

I'm getting old. When I squeeze into a tight parking space, I'm sexually satisfied for the day.

Rodney Dangerfield

Sex and death. Two things that come once in a lifetime. But at least after death you are not nauseous.

Woody Allen

Use it or lose it.

Joan Collins

I haven't had sex since 1959. Of course it's only 21:00 now.

Tom O'Connor

My sex life is now reduced to fan letters from an elderly lesbian who wants to borrow 800 dollars.

Groucho Marx

If it weren't for speed bumps, pickpockets and frisking at airports, I'd have no sex life at all.

Rodney Dangerfield

Nowadays I reserve my sexual activities for special occasions – such as the installation of a new Pope.

Dave Barry

If it wasn't for the rectal probe I'd have no sex life at all.

Barry Cryer

After 50, litigation takes the place of sex.

Gore Vidal

—Your fly-buttons are undone.
—No matter. The dead bird does not fall out of the nest.

Winston Churchill

As a young man, I used to have four supple members and one stiff one. Now I have four stiff and one supple.

Henri Duc D'Aumale

I'm going to Iowa to collect an award. Then I'm appearing at Carnegie Hall; it's sold out. Then I'm sailing to France to pick up an honour from the French government. I'd give it all up for one erection.

Groucho Marx

To succeed with the opposite sex, tell her you're impotent. She can't wait to disprove it.

Cary Grant, 72

If the devil were to offer me a resurgence of what is commonly called virility, I'd decline. 'Just keep my liver and lungs in good working order,' I'd reply, 'so I can go on drinking and smoking.'

Luis Buñuel

A medical report states that the human male is physically capable of enjoying sex up to and even beyond the age of 80. Not as a participant of course...

Denis Norden

Sex after 90 is like trying to shoot pool with a rope. I'm at that age now where just putting my cigar in its holder is a thrill.

George Burns

Like being unchained from a lunatic.

Sophocles on his declining sexual powers

Lord, give me chastity – but not yet.

St Augustine

I know nothing about sex because I was always married.

Zsa Zsa Gabor

Before we make love my husband takes a painkiller.

Joan Rivers

The Three Ages of Marriage: 20 is when you watch the TV after. Forty is when you watch the TV during. Sixty is when you watch the TV instead.

Anon

Sex

After a man passes 60, his mischief is mainly in his head.

Washington Irving

Men of my age are just too old, and the younger ones may have the energy but they don't have the intellect.

Cilla Black

You know you're getting older when you have sex with someone half your age and it's legal.

Dan Savage

Statistics show that at the age of 70, there are five women to every man. Isn't that the darnedest time for a guy to get those odds?

Anon

The longer thread of life we spin
The more occasion still to sin.

Robert Herrick

When a girl's under 21 she's protected by the law. When she is over 65, she's protected by nature and anywhere in between, she's fair game.

Cary Grant

What is a younger woman? I'm pretty old, so almost every woman is younger than me.

Jack Nicholson

It seems that after the age of 50, I began to age at the rate of about three years per year. I began falling asleep 15 minutes into an episode of *Seinfeld*. I also began falling asleep during sex rather than after.

Anon

When they were asked what they thought of a phone mast being erected on the adjacent military museum, one 97-year-old raised his hand to ask, 'Will it make us sterile?'

General Sir Jeremy MacKenzie, referring to a Chelsea pensioner

You still chase women, but only downhill.

Bob Hope, on turning 70

The pleasures that once were heaven, look silly at 67.

Noël Coward

Now that I'm over 60, I'm veering towards respectability.

Shelley Winters

I'm still a terrible flirt. It boosts your ego knowing you still have the ability, but that's as far as it goes. Now we have a silly rule – no hands in jumpers.

Antony Worrall Thompson

Sex

If you can't have fun as an ageing sex symbol when you hit 60, I don't know what will become of you.

Raquel Welch

I'm not a raver any more. All good things must come to an end.

Jack Nicholson

You don't get older. You get better.

Shirley Bassey

My wild oats have turned to shredded wheat.

Anon

How exciting! This is the first time I've ever been implicated in a sex case. I don't remember handling her breasts. We were just having lunch.

Antony Worrall Thompson, on being accused of having an affair

Mary Wesley has thick white hair, endless legs and the captivating face that made her such a sexy beauty in her youth. Next year she will be 90, which she finds rather irritating because there is nothing elderly about her.

Lynda Lee-Potter

My love life is terrible. The last time I was inside a woman was when I visited the Statue of Liberty.

Woody Allen

I have so little sex appeal that my gynaecologist calls me 'sir'.

Joan Rivers

Clinton lied. A man might forget where he parks or where he lives, but he never forgets oral sex, no matter how bad it is.

Barbara Bush

I'm a different guy here in my 60s. I don't have the same libido. It used to be that I didn't think I could go to sleep if I wasn't involved in some kind of amorous contact. Well, I spend a lot of time sleeping alone these days.

Jack Nicholson

In my next life I'm going to come back as a rather good-looking, even quite fat and plain 50-year-old man, who's just been widowed or sadly divorced, and I would go to the country and I would clean up. I would get a bonk every night of the week.

Jilly Cooper, Grumpy Old Women

Sex appeal is in your heart and head. I'll be sexy no matter how old or how my body changes.

Sonia Braga

Sex

One of the best parts of growing older? You can flirt all you like since you've become harmless.

Liz Smith

Getting older is all about high blood pressure, high cholesterol, high anxiety and low sex drive. At my age, 'safe sex' is not falling out of bed.

Anon

It's been so long since I've had sex I've forgotten who ties up whom.

Joan Rivers

There are a number of mechanical devices which increase sexual arousal, particularly in women. Chief among these is the Mercedes-Benz 380SL convertible.

P.J. O'Rourke

I had wanted for years to get Mrs Thatcher in front of my camera … as she got more powerful she got sort of sexier.

Helmut Newton

In my outrageous 20s, I asked a charming, chatty Englishwoman I'd met in Villefranche when people stopped having sex. 'It's no good asking me, my dear,' she said. 'I'm only 83.'

Anon

I once had a rose named after me and I was very flattered. But I was not pleased to read the description in the catalogue: no good in a bed, but fine up against a wall.

Eleanor Roosevelt

I was with this girl the other night and from the way she was responding to my skilful caresses, you would have sworn that she was conscious from the top of her head to the tag on her toes.

Emo Philips

My grandmother's 90; she's dating a man 93. They never argue: they can't hear each other.

Cathy Ladman

Having sex at my age is still wonderful, really. It just gets more difficult to see with whom you are having it.

Anon

I'd Rather Have a Cup of Tea

Growing old is when you resent the swimsuit issue of *Sports Illustrated* because there are fewer articles to read.

George Burns

I'd Rather Have a Cup of Tea

Everyone probably thinks that I'm a raving nymphomaniac, that I have an insatiable sexual appetite, when the truth is I'd rather read a book.

Madonna

Middle age is having a choice of two temptations and choosing the one that will get you home earlier.

Dan Bennett

Now that I think of it, I wish I had been a hell-raiser when I was 30 years old. I tried it when I was 50 but I always got sleepy.

Groucho Marx

My wife is a sex object. Every time I ask for sex, she objects.

Les Dawson

I only watch *Baywatch* for the articles.

Chief Dan

They say marriages are made in Heaven. But so is thunder and lightning.

Clint Eastwood

I don't want to snog old men, with their yellow horrible teeth, old crinkly skin and hairy moles.

Cilla Black

Thank God! Now I realise I've been chained to an idiot for the last 60 years of my life!

Kingsley Amis at 70, on his lost libido

The important thing in acting is to be able to laugh and cry. If I have to cry, I think of my sex life. If I have to laugh, I think of my sex life.

Glenda Jackson

I haven't had sex in eight months. To be honest, I now prefer to go bowling.

Anon

As I get older, I just prefer to knit.

Tracey Ullman

I'm at the age where I want two girls. In case I fall asleep they will have someone to talk to.

Rodney Dangerfield

Sex is a bad thing because it rumples the clothes.

Jackie Onassis

I am happy now that Charles calls on my bedchamber less frequently than of old. As it is, I now endure but two calls a week and when I hear his steps outside my door I lie down on my bed, close my eyes, open my legs and think of England.

Lady Alice Hillingdon

All this fuss about sleeping together. For physical pleasure I'd sooner go to my dentist any day.

Evelyn Waugh

My wife only has sex with me for a purpose. Last night it was to time an egg.

Rodney Dangerfield

Viva Viagra

I only take Viagra when I am with more than one woman.

Jack Nicholson

Sex at the age of 84 is a wonderful experience. Especially the one in the winter.

Milton Berle

There is more money being spent on breast implants and Viagra than on Alzheimer's research. This means that by 2030, there should be a large elderly population with perky boobs and huge erections and absolutely no recollection of what to do with them.

Anon

At my age, I'm envious of a stiff wind.

Rodney Dangerfield

Everything that goes up must come down. But there comes a time when not everything that's down can come up.

George Burns

An elderly gentleman went to the local drugstore and asked the pharmacist for Viagra. The pharmacist said, 'That's no problem. How many do you want?' The man replied, 'Just a few, maybe half a dozen, but can you cut each one into four pieces?' The pharmacist said, 'That's too small a dose. That won't get you through sex.' The gentleman said, 'Oh, that's all right. I'm past 80 years old, and I don't even think about sex any more. I just want it to stick out far enough so I don't pee on my shoes.'

Anon

Look at Catherine Zeta-Jones and Michael Douglas. She's a clever girl, because like me, she knows that an older man has time to love and nurture you.

Celine Dion

Viva Viagra

Bob Dole revealed he is one of the test subjects for Viagra. He said on Larry King, 'I wish I had bought stock in it.' Only a Republican would think the best part of Viagra is the fact that you could make money off of it.'

Jay Leno

If I marry again at my age, I'll go on honeymoon to Viagra Falls.

George Burns

An elderly man goes to confession and says to the priest, 'Father, I'm 80 years old, married, have four kids and 11 grandchildren. I started taking Viagra and last night I had an affair and made love to two 18-year-old girls. Both of them. Twice.'

The priest said: 'Well, my son, when was the last time you were in confession?'

'Never, Father, I'm Jewish.'

'So then, why are you telling me?'

'Heck! I'm telling everybody!'

Anon

Work

In the days when I went to work, I never once knew what I was doing. These days, I never work. Work does age one so.

Quentin Crisp

Age to me means nothing. I can't get old while I'm working. I was old when I was 21 and out of work. As long as you're working, you stay young.

George Burns

If you keep working you'll last longer and I just want to keep vertical. I'd hate to spend the rest of my life trying to outwit an 18-inch fish.

Harold S. Geneen

I'm too old for a paper round, too young for social security and too tired for an affair.

Erma Bombeck

I am delighted to find that even at my age great ideas come to me, the pursuit and development of which should require another lifetime.

Johann Wolfgang von Goethe

Very few people do anything creative after the age of 35. The reason is that very few people do anything creative before the age of 35.

Joel Hildebrand

Like the old pro said, it's not the work, it's the stairs.

Elaine Stritch

How can I die? I'm booked!

George Burns

The Gold Watch

RETIREMENT

I'm taking early retirement. I want my share of Social Security before the whole system goes bust.

David Letterman

I have made enough noise in the world already, perhaps too much, and am now getting old, and want retirement.

Napoleon Bonaparte

It is time I stepped aside for a less experienced and less able man.

Scott Elledge

When a man falls into his anecdotage, it is a sign for him to retire from the world.

Benjamin Disraeli

I really think that it's better to retire, in Uncle Earl's terms, when you still have some snap left in your garters.

Russell B. Long

I know how we'll end up in our dotage – my cat, Vienna, stretched across a tennis racket, and me in the local library clinging to the radiators.

Rigsby, Rising Damp

Abolish the retirement age. After all, if everyone had to stop working when they reached 65, Winston Churchill would not have been our wartime leader. He was 66 when he became Prime Minister.

Daily Mirror

We spend our lives on the run. We get up by the clock, eat and sleep by the clock, get up again, go to work, and then we retire. And what do they give us? A bloody clock.

Dave Allen

The Gold Watch

Sometimes it's better to be sacked. I hate the leaving do, and the statutory retirement present, which is always something awful like a gold watch or an engraved wok.

Greg Dyke

Musicians don't retire; they stop when there's no more music in them.

Louis Armstrong

I'll never retire. I won't quit the business until I get run over by a truck, a producer or a critic.

Jack Lemmon

Retire? Did Christ come down from the Cross?

Pope John Paul II

There comes a time when it is too late to retire.

Lord Hailsham

I'm retired. I'm now officially a lower form of life than a Duracell battery. I've been replaced by a box. It's standard procedure apparently for a man my age. The next stage is to stick you inside one.

Victor Meldrew, One Foot in the Grave

After I retired, I fished a lot, dove a lot, boated a lot – and made Johnny Walker Red about a quarter of a million dollars richer.

Dennis Diaz

What do gardeners do when they retire?

Bob Monkhouse

What shall I do now I'm retired? I thought I might grow a beard … give me something to do.

Victor Meldrew, One Foot in the Grave

I make the coffee, Barbara makes the beds, and we're right back to square one where we got married when we were 20 years old.

George Bush, former US President

My husband has just retired. I married him for better or for worse, but not for lunch.

Hazel Weiss

A retired husband is often a wife's full-time job.

Ella Harris

The Gold Watch

If I had to retire I'd probably bore my wife to tears. The commonest sight, now that people retire earlier and live much longer, is of couples walking round supermarkets, the wives filling the trolleys, the men carrying lists and saying: 'Why are you buying this?'

Terry Wogan

It's very hard to make a home for a man if he's always in it.

Winifred Kirkland

The important thing about women today is, as they get older, they still keep house. It's one reason why they don't die, but men die when they retire. Women just polish the teacups.

Margaret Mead

I don't even think about a retirement programme because I'm working for the Lord, for the Almighty. And even though the Lord's pay isn't very high, his retirement programme is, you might say, out of this world.

George Foreman

Retirement at 65 is ridiculous. When I was 65 I still had pimples.

George Burns

Never retire. Michelangelo was carving the *Rondanini* just before he died at 89. Verdi finished his opera *Falstaff* at 80. And the 80-year-old artist Goya scrawled on a drawing, 'I am still learning'.

Dr W. Gifford-Jones

On announcing his retirement: You can only milk a cow for so long, then you're left holding the pail.

Hank Aaron

I'm mad, you know? I don't think of retiring at all.

Paul McCartney

People are always asking me when I'm going to retire. Why should I? I'm still making movies, and I'm a senior citizen, so I can see myself at half price.

George Burns

This is my final word. It is time for me to become an apprentice once more. I have not settled in which direction. But somewhere, sometime, soon.

Lord Beaverbrook, taken from his last public statement

I don't want to retire. I'm not that good at crossword puzzles.

Norman Mailer

The Gold Watch

When old, retire from work, but not from life.

M.K. Soni

If youth is wasted on the young, then retirement is wasted on the old.

Anon

Retire? I'm going to stay in show business until I'm the only one left.

George Burns, age 90

At 85 you can only think ahead for the next 50 years or so.

Chuck Jones, on signing a long-term contract with Warner Brothers

Don't retire, retread!

Robert Otterbourg

Retirement is the period when you exchange the bills in your wallet for snapshots of your grandchildren.

Anon

It's been different. I started driving again. I started cooking again. My driving's better than my cooking. George has discovered Sam's Club.

Barbara Bush

When a man retires and time is no longer a matter of urgent importance, his colleagues generally present him with a watch.

R.C. Sherriff

Retirement: That's when you return from work one day and say, 'Hi, honey, I'm home – forever.'

Gene Perret

You're 65 today – and it's the first day of the rest of your life savings.

Anon

Retirement? You're talking about death, right?

Robert Altman

Retirement kills more people than hard work ever did.

Malcolm Forbes

The trouble with retirement is that you never get a day off.

Abe Lemons

I'm retired – goodbye tension, hello pension!

Anon

The Gold Watch

When a man retires, his wife gets twice the husband but only half the income.

Chi Chi Rodriguez

Retired is being twice tired, I've thought. First tired of working, then tired of not.

Richard Armour

Retirement: It's nice to get out of the rat race, but you have to learn to get along with less cheese.

Gene Perret

I love working. It's what I do best, and if I didn't work and tried to slow down, I'd just become a boring old fart.

Rik Mayall

Middle age is when work is a lot less fun and fun is a lot more work.

Anon

O, blest retirement! friend to life's decline –
How blest is he who crowns, in shades like these,
A youth of labour with an age of ease!

Oliver Goldsmith

Retirement is wonderful. It's doing nothing without worrying about getting caught at it.

Gene Perret

There are some who start their retirement long before they stop working.

Robert Half

The question isn't at what age I want to retire, it's at what income.

George Foreman

The challenge of retirement is how to spend time without spending money.

Anon

Once it was impossible to find any Bond villains older than myself, I retired.

Roger Moore

Retirement means no pressure, no stress, no heartache … unless you play golf.

Gene Perret

Retirement must be wonderful. I mean, you can suck in your stomach for only so long.

Burt Reynolds

Time Flies

When you retire, think and act as if you were still working; when you're still working, think and act a bit as if you were already retired.

Anon

I've been trying for some time to develop a lifestyle that doesn't require my presence.

Gary Trudeau

Retirement - now life begins.

Catherine Pulsifer

Time Flies

One day, aged 45, I just went into the kitchen to make myself a cup of tea, and when I came out I found I was 68.

Thora Hird

One day a bachelor, the next a grandpa. What is the secret of the trick? How did I get so old so quick?

Ogden Nash

As I get older the years just fly by. I don't think there was an April this year.

Jeremy Hardy

Years grow shorter but days grow longer. When you're over 70, a day is an awful lot of time.

Carl Sandburg

Guinness is a great day-shortener. If you get out of bed first thing and drink a glass then the day doesn't begin until about 12.30, when you come to again, which is nice. I try to live in a perpetual snooze.

Quentin Crisp

Men talk of killing time, while time quietly kills them.

Dion Boucicault

Half our life is spent trying to find something to do with the time we have rushed through life trying to save.

Will Rogers

No matter how much time you save, at the end of your life, there's no extra time saved up. You'll be going, 'What do you mean there's no time? I had a microwave oven, Velcro sneakers, a clip-on tie. Where's the time?' But there isn't any. Because when you waste time in life, they subtract it. Like if you saw all the *Rocky* movies, they deduct that.

Jerry Seinfeld

Time Flies

There is never enough time, unless you're serving it.

Malcolm Forbes

Whenever I get down about life going by too quickly, what helps me is a little mantra that I repeat to myself: at least I'm not a fruit fly.

Ray Romano

Don't be over-impressed by time. Accept it, but don't kowtow to it. We should still be able to stick two fingers in the air as the diminishing amount of sand trickles through the hourglass.

George Melly

This is your life and it's ending one minute at a time.

David Fincher

Time is a great teacher, but unfortunately it kills all its pupils.

Hector Berlioz

I have decided that Father Time doesn't come after everybody with a scythe. He has come to me often with a pair of tweezers – he takes a little nip here and then a little nip there and I'm sure that eventually he'll have all of me.

Anon

Tobacco, coffee, alcohol, hashish, prussic acid, strychnine, are weak dilutions: the surest poison is time.

Ralph Waldo Emerson

Those of you in your 20s have the feeling that time is something of which you have an endless supply. Again, take it from someone who has been on this planet a good deal longer than most of you have, that is not the case.

Chief Justice William H. Rehnquist

Senescence begins and middle age ends the day your descendants outnumber your friends.

Ogden Nash

You can't leave footprints in the sands of time if you're sitting on your butt. And who wants to leave butt-prints in the sands of time?

Anon

I want to go ahead of Father Time with a scythe of my own.

H. G. Wells

Every girl should use what Mother Nature gave her before Father Time takes it away.

Laurence J. Peter

Yes, time flies. And where did it leave you? Old too soon, smart too late.

Mike Tyson

Life Is...

...like a sewer. What you get out of it depends on what you put into it.

Tom Lehrer

...like a play: it's not the length, but the excellence of the acting that matters.

Seneca

...the art of drawing without an eraser.

Anon

...the art of drawing sufficient conclusions from insufficient data.

Samuel Butler

...a sexually transmitted disease and the mortality rate is 100 per cent.

R.D. Laing

...something that happens when you can't get to sleep.

Fran Lebowitz

...hard. After all, it kills you.

Katharine Hepburn

...like playing a violin solo in public and learning the instrument as one goes on.

Samuel Butler

...a tragedy when seen in close-up, but a comedy in long-shot.

Charlie Chaplin

...a long lesson in humility.

James M. Barrie

...like a taxi. The meter just keeps a-ticking whether you are getting somewhere or just standing still.

Lou Erickso

...a succession of lessons which must be lived to be understood.

Ralph Waldo Emerson

...wasted on the living.

Douglas Adams

...like a roll of toilet paper: long and useful, but it always ends at the wrong moment.

Anon

Life Is...

Life can be wildly tragic at times, and I've had my share. But whatever happens to you, you have to keep a slightly comic attitude. In the final analysis, you have got not to forget to laugh.

Katharine Hepburn

What you have to do in life is not look back at all the grievances but look forward to what is ahead.

Terry Waite

All I can say about life is, Oh God, enjoy it!

Bob Newhart

He felt that his whole life was some kind of dream and he sometimes wondered whose it was and whether they were enjoying it.

Douglas Adams

I hope life isn't a big joke, because I don't get it.

Jack Handey

I long ago came to the conclusion that all life is six to five against.

Damon Runyon

You suddenly realise that life moves at an incredible speed. When I take my granddaughter to Hampstead

Heath I go to the same places I used to take her father. It just seems that life has telescoped.

Anon

The evening of a well-spent life brings its lamps with it.

Joseph Joubert

The average man, who does not know what to do with his life, wants another one which will last forever.

Anatole France

Carpe Diem

When one subtracts from life infancy (which is vegetation), sleep, eating and swilling, buttoning and unbuttoning – how much remains of downright existence? The summer of a dormouse.

Lord Byron

For every person who has ever lived there has come, at last, a spring he will never see. Glory then in the springs that are yours.

Pam Brown

Carpe Diem

Life will be over sooner than we think. If we have bikes to ride and people to love, now is the time.

Elisabeth Kübler-Ross

If you were going to die soon and had only one phone call you could make, who would you call and what would you say? And why are you waiting?

Stephen Levine

Most of us spend our lives as if we had another one in the bank.

Ben Irwin

One of the most tragic things I know about human nature is that all of us tend to put off living. We are all dreaming of some magical rose garden over the horizon – instead of enjoying the roses that are blooming outside our windows today.

Dale Carnegie

Even a great feast has a last course.

Chinese proverb

At 87, 'someday' and 'one of these days' are losing their grip on my vocabulary; if it's worth seeing or hearing or doing, I want to see and hear and do it now.

Anon

Don't ever save anything for a special occasion. Being alive is the special occasion.

Avril Sloe

Don't save things 'for best'. Drink that vintage bottle of wine – from your best crystal glasses. Wear your best designer jacket to go down to the post office to collect your pension. And, every morning, spritz yourself with that perfume you save for parties.

Geraldine Mayer

I've decided life is too fragile to finish a book I dislike just because it cost $16.95 and everyone else loved it. Or eat a fried egg with a broken yolk (which I hate) when the dog would leap over the St Louis Arch for it.

Erma Bombeck

Life is too short to learn German.

Richard Porson

Dust if you must, but wouldn't it be better,
To paint a picture or write a letter,
Bake a cake or plant a seed,
Ponder the difference between want and need?

Dust if you must, but there's not much time,
With rivers to swim and mountains to climb,

Carpe Diem

Music to hear and books to read,
Friends to cherish and life to lead.

Dust if you must, but the world's out there,
With the sun in your eyes, the wind in your hair,
A flutter of snow, a shower of rain.
This day will not come 'round again.

Dust if you must, but bear in mind,
Old age will come and it's not always kind.
And when you go and go you must,
You, yourself, will make more dust.

Anon

Don't spend your life trying to please those who won't cry at your funeral.

Gerald Brooks

Don't wait for pie in the sky when you die. Get yours now, with ice cream on top!

The Reverend Ike

Enjoy yourself; it's later than you think.

Horace

Gotta Lotta Livin' To Do

There will come a time when you believe everything is finished. That will be the beginning.

Louis L'Amour

I want to tell people approaching and perhaps fearing age that it is a time of discovery. If they say, 'Of what?' I can only answer, 'We must find out for ourselves, otherwise it won't be a discovery.'

Florida Scott-Maxwell

Look, I don't want to wax philosophic, but I will say that if you're alive you've got to flap your arms and legs, you've got to jump around a lot, for life is the very opposite of death, and therefore you must at very least think noisy and colourfully, or you're not alive.

Mel Brooks

Let's not go out and get denture cream. Let's go to the nude beach and let our wrinkled selves hang out! We'll sit on the boardwalk and watch the old men rearrange themselves when they come out of the water.

Sophia Petrillo, The Golden Girls

Gotta Lotta Livin' To Do

Do not grow old, no matter how long you live. Never cease to stand like curious children before the Great Mystery into which we were born.

Albert Einstein

I am more alive than most people. I am an electric eel in a pond of goldfish.

Edith Sitwell

When you're young, you don't know, but you don't know you don't know, so you take some chances. In your 20s and 30s you don't know, and you know you don't know, and that tends to freeze you: less risk-taking. In your 40s you know, but you don't know you know, so you may still be a little tentative. But then, as you pass 50, if you've been paying attention, you know, and you know you know. Time for some fun.

George Carlin

Life is a great big canvas, and you should throw all the paint on it you can.

Danny Kaye

Write, paint, sculpt, learn the piano, take up dancing, whether it's the tango or line-dancing, start a college course, fall in love all over again – the possibilities are limitless for you to achieve your private ambitions.

Joan Collins

Singing, fishing, meeting my close and dear friends, looking at pictures and nature, shocking a few people who deserve shocking, taking my pills, writing a book and swigging Irish whiskey. These are my ways of fending off the old gent with the scythe waiting patiently to harvest me.

George Melly

I use my increased leisure time to look at paintings wherever there is a gallery, to enjoy opera and drama at a theatre, to visit country houses.

Denis Healey

Life isn't measured by how many breaths we take, but by the moments that take our breath away.

Chinese saying

Sometimes I would rather have someone take away years of my life than take away a moment.

Pearl Bailey

We should do something that will make your heart dance once a day. If you can't do that because you're too depressed, then do something that will make somebody else's heart dance.

Yoko Ono

Gotta Lotta Livin' To Do

There were days last winter when I danced for sheer joy out in my frost-bound garden in spite of my years and children. But I did it behind a bush, having a due regard for the decencies.

Elizabeth von Arnim

I get up before anyone else in my household, not because sleep has deserted me in my advancing years, but because an intense eagerness to live draws me from my bed.

Maurice Goudeket

Most people say that as you get old, you have to give up things. I think you get old because you give up things.

Theodore Green

Develop interest in life as you see it: in people, things, literature, music – the world is so rich, simply throbbing with treasures, beautiful souls and interesting people. Forget yourself.

Henry Miller

I wouldn't mind turning into vermilion goldfish.

Henri Matisse, 80

Enjoying sex, loving fashion, having fun, decorating our homes, going on lavish holidays – the list is endless. Onward!

Joan Collins

It is a mistake to regard age as a downhill grade towards dissolution. The reverse is true. As one grows older, one climbs with surprising strides.

George Sand

You have to take time out to be old. I'm still full of piss and vinegar.

Paul Newman

If old people were to mobilize en masse they would constitute a formidable fighting force, as anyone who has ever had the temerity to try to board a bus ahead of a little old lady with an umbrella well knows.

Vera Forrester

I work every day and I want to die shouting *Mierda*!

Joan Miró

I can't actually see myself putting make-up on my face at the age of 60. But I can see myself going on a camel train to Samarkand.

Glenda Jackson, actress

Gotta Lotta Livin' To Do

At past 50, I solemnly and painfully learned to ride the bicycle.

Henry Adams

You should make a point of trying every experience once, excepting incest and folk-dancing.

Anon

I hope I have a young outlook. Since I have an old everything else, this is my one chance of having a bit of youth as a part of me.

Richard Armour

In a boat I lost 20 or 30 years straight away.

Helen Tew, 89, transatlantic sailor

The only time I've ever been rendered speechless with fury was when some daft television presenter opened a programme aimed at senior travellers by asking what sort of holidays were 'suitable' for them. 'Any and all they really want to take' is the short answer.

Elisabeth de Stroumillo

Cruising: if you thought you didn't like people on land…

Carol Leifer

Signs You're on a Bad Cruise: the brochure boasts the ship was the subject of a *60 Minutes* exposé; as you board, a personal injury lawyer hands you his business card; no matter what you order from the bar, it tastes of salt; every time you see the crew, they're wearing life-jackets; the vessel's name is the *S.S. Scurvy*.

David Letterman

I'd like to learn to ski but I'm 44 and I'm worried about my knees. They creak a lot and I'm afraid they might start an avalanche.

Jonathan Ross

I now realise that the small hills you see on ski-slopes are formed around the bodies of 47-year-olds who tried to learn snowboarding.

Dave Barry

There isn't anybody who doesn't like to see an old man make a comeback. Jimmy Connors seemed like a jerk to me until he was 40. After that, I rooted for him all the time. How could you not?

T. Boone Pickens

Golfers grow old and try to shoot their age. It must be a terrific feeling when someone asks your age and you can say, 'Par.'

The Pittsburgh Post

Gotta Lotta Livin' To Do

The older you get, the stronger the wind gets – and it's always in your face.

Jack Nicklaus

You're never too old. A person of 60 can grow as much as a child of 6. Michelangelo did some of his best paintings when past 80; George Bernard Shaw was still writing plays at 90; Grandma Moses didn't even begin painting until she was 79.

Maxwell Naltz

I don't want to get to the end of my life and find that I lived just the length of it. I want to have lived the width of it as well.

Diane Ackerman

Life is either a daring adventure, or nothing.

Helen Keller

Dance as if no one were watching, sing as if no one were listening, and live every day as if it were your last.

Tish Provest

Do not go gently into that good night,
Old age should burn and rage at close of day…

Dylan Thomas

There is sleeping enough in the grave.

Irish saying

Writing the Memoirs

Keep a diary, and someday it'll keep you.

Mae West

I was born because it was a habit in those days. People didn't know anything else.

Will Rogers

My father had a profound influence on me – he was a lunatic.

Spike Milligan

I used to think I was an interesting person, but I must tell you how sobering a thought it is to realise your life's story fills about 35 pages and you have, actually, not much to say.

Roseanne Barr

I wanted to be President of the United States. I really did. The older I get, the less preposterous the idea seems.

Alec Baldwin

Writing the Memoirs

Thank goodness I was never sent to school: it would have rubbed off some of the originality.

Beatrix Potter

I succeeded by saying what everyone else is thinking.

Joan Rivers

I wrote the story myself. It's about a girl who lost her reputation and never missed it.

Mae West

Each has his past shut in him like the leaves of a book known to him by his heart, and his friends can only read the title.

Virginia Woolf

When I was growing up, there were two things that were unpopular in my house. One was me, and the other was my guitar.

Bruce Springsteen

I wasn't as smart then as I am now. But who ever is?

Tina Turner

When I realised what I had turned out to be was a lousy, two-bit pool hustler and a drunk, I wasn't depressed at all. I was glad to have a profession.

Danny McGoorty, Irish pool player

In my 20s, my pleasures tended to be physical. In my 30s, my pleasures tended to be intellectual. I can't say which was more exquisite.

Steve Kangas

I always wanted to be an explorer, but – it seemed I was doomed to be nothing more than a very silly person.

Michael Palin

I have never described the time I was in *Doctor Who* as anything except a kind of ecstatic success, but all the rest has been rather a muddle and a disappointment. Compared to *Doctor Who*, it has been an outrageous failure really – it's so boring.

Tom Baker

I'm writing an unauthorized autobiography.

Steven Wright

I don't think anyone should write his autobiography until after he's dead.

Samuel Goldwyn

An autobiography is an obituary in serial form with the last instalment missing.

Quentin Crisp

Writing the Memoirs

Rebecca was a busy liar in her distinguished old age, reinventing her past for gullible biographers.

Walter Clemons, on Rebecca West

All I ever seemed to get was the kind of girl who had a special dispensation from Rome to wear the thickest part of her legs below the knee.

Hugh Leonard

I couldn't wait for success, so I went on ahead without it.

Jonathan Winters

I spent 90 per cent of my money on women and drink. The rest I wasted.

George Best

On what?

Chris Eubank, when asked if he had ever thought of writing an autobiography

I always knew looking back on my tears would bring me laughter, but I never knew looking back on my laughter would make me cry.

Cat Stevens

Forty pictures I was in, and all I remember is 'What kind of bra will you be wearing today, honey?' That was always the area of big decision – from the neck to the navel.

Donna Reed

The really good idea is always traceable back quite a long way, often to a not very good idea which sparked off another idea that was only slightly better, which somebody else misunderstood in such a way that they then said something which was really rather interesting.

John Cleese

My toughest fight was with my first wife, and she won every round.

Muhammad Ali

It was no great tragedy being Judy Garland's daughter. I had tremendously interesting childhood years – except they had little to do with being a child.

Liza Minnelli

This is the second most bizarre thing ever to happen to me. The first was when I was sued by a woman who claimed she became pregnant because she watched me on TV and I bent her contraceptive coil.

Uri Geller

Writing the Memoirs

This bikini made me a success.

Ursula Andress

I wanted revenge; I wanted to dance on the graves of a few people who made me unhappy. It's a pretty infantile way to go through life – I'll show them – but I've done it, and I've got more than I ever dreamed of.

Anthony Hopkins

I sold the memoirs of my sex life to a publisher – they are going to make a board game out of it.

Woody Allen

I grew up in Europe, where the history comes from.

Eddie Izzard

I was coming home from kindergarten – well, they told me it was kindergarten. I found out later I had been working in a factory for ten years. It's good for a kid to know how to make gloves.

Ellen DeGeneres

Success didn't spoil me. I've always been insufferable.

Fran Lebowitz

My childhood was a period of waiting for the moment when I could send everyone and everything connected with it to hell.

Igor Stravinsky

I can't understand why I flunked American history. When I was a kid there was so little of it.

George Burns

There is nothing that makes you so aware of the improvisation of human existence as a song unfinished or an old address book.

Carson McCullers

I didn't really say everything I said.

Yogi Berra

It took me 15 years to discover I had no talent for writing, but I couldn't give it up, because by that time I was too famous.

Robert Benchley

History will be kind to me for I intend to write it.

Winston Churchill

There used to be a real me, but I had it surgically removed.

Peter Sellers

Writing the Memoirs

Acting is merely the art of keeping a large group of people from coughing.

Sir Ralph Richardson

As a kid, I knew I wanted to be either a cartoonist or an astronaut. The latter was never much of a possibility, as I don't even like riding in elevators.

Bill Watterson

The most important thing I would learn in school was that almost everything I would learn in school would be utterly useless. When I was 15 I knew the principal industries of the Ruhr Valley, the underlying causes of World War I and what Peig Sayers had for her dinner every day ... What I wanted to know when I was 15 was the best way to chat up girls. That is what I still want to know.

Joseph O'Connor, The Secret World of the Irish Male

If I'd only known, I would have been a locksmith.

Albert Einstein

A Quiet Life

I once wanted to save the world. Now I just want to leave the room with some dignity.

Lotus Weinstock

As I grow old, I find myself less and less inclined to take the stairs two at a time.

Bernard Baruch

I turn 70 this year and all of a sudden the horizon that once seemed far away looms right there in front of you. You feel an irresistible urge to slow down, to take your foot off the accelerator, touch it to the brake – gently, but surely – and start negotiating yourself out of the fast lane.

Bill Moyers, former White House Press Secretary

I am 72 years of age, at which period there comes over one a shameful love of ease and repose, common to dogs, horses, clergymen and even to Edinburgh reviewers. Then an idea comes across me that I am entitled to five or six years of quiet before I die.

Rev. Sydney Smith

Even under a harsh God, one is entitled to serenity in old age.

Albert Outler

A Quiet Life

What is wrong with settling down with a good book into a rocking chair by the fireside, wearing a comfy pair of slippers if that is what makes you happy?

Eloise Pagett

I love this time of day. When I'm sitting here in my own little home, with my own wonderful little hubby, and we talk about issues of the day and discuss world affairs and generally just snuggle.

Mavis Wilton, Coronation Street

I used to have a sign over my computer that read, 'Old Dogs Can Learn New Tricks', but lately I sometimes ask myself how many more tricks I want to learn. Wouldn't it be easier to be outdated?

Ram Dass

If old age in the shape of waning strength says to me often, 'Thou shalt not!', so do my years smile upon me and say to me, 'Thou needst not!'

Mary Vorse

It's only natural that a person becomes quieter as they grow older. They've got more to keep quiet about.

Samuel Butler

One's first step to wisdom is to question everything – and one's last is to come to terms with everything.

Georg Christoph Lichtenberg

Growing older, I have lost the need to be political, which means, in this country, the need to be left. I am driven into grudging toleration of the Conservative Party because it is the party of non-politics, of resistance to politics.

Kingsley Amis

When one has reached 81, one likes to sit back and let the world turn by itself, without trying to push it.

Sean O'Casey

The members seated in the pavilion at the Test Match declined to join in the Mexican Wave. Well, when you get to a certain age, every time you just get out of your chair, it's a bit of an adventure.

Henry Blofeld

Old men are dangerous; it doesn't matter to them what is going to happen to the world.

George Bernard Shaw

Rest is not idleness, and to lie sometimes on the grass on a summer day listening to the murmur of water, or watching the clouds float across the sky, is hardly a waste of time.

John Lubbock

I shall be 70 in two months' time and feel exactly as I did when I was 20. I was idle and indolent then, and little has changed in the past 50 years except that perhaps now I am better at getting away with it.

Arnold Thomson

Life Is a Cruise

My parents didn't want to move to Florida, but they turned 60, and that's the law.

Jerry Seinfeld

I love flying. I've been to almost as many places as my luggage.

Bob Hope

You haven't lived until you've died in California.

Mort Sahl

They invented the three-day bank holiday weekend because you can't lump all the bad weather into just Saturday and Sunday.

Anon

The great and recurring question about abroad is, is it worth getting there?

Rose Macaulay

Abroad is unutterably bloody and foreigners are fiends.

Nancy Mitford

The scientific theory I like best is that the rings of Saturn are composed entirely of lost airline luggage.

Mark Russell

I don't hold with abroad and think foreigners speak English when our backs are turned.

Quentin Crisp

I wouldn't mind seeing China if I could come back the same day.

Philip Larkin

I hate vacations. There's nothing to do.

David Mamet

I also hate those holidays that fall on a Monday where you don't get mail, those fake holidays like Columbus Day. What did Christopher Columbus do, discover America? If he hadn't, somebody else would have and we'd still be here. Big deal.

John Waters

I said I didn't want to spend most of my life in Holiday Inns, but I've checked and they've all been redecorated. They're marvellous places to stay and I've thought it over and that's where I'd like to be.

Walter F. Mondale

Some national parks have long waiting lists for camping reservations. When you have to wait a year to sleep next to a tree, something is wrong.

George Carlin

Geriatric Gardening

To get the best results you must talk to your vegetables.

Prince Charles

Though an old man, I am but a young gardener.

Thomas Jefferson

I want Death to find me planting my cabbages.

Michel De Montaigne

Planting is one of my great amusements, and even of those things which can only be for posterity, for a Septuagenary has no right to count on any thing but annuals.

Thomas Jefferson

If you want to be happy for a short time, get drunk; happy for a long time, fall in love; happy forever, take up gardening.

Arthur Smith

Live each day as if it were your last,
and garden as though you will live forever.

Anon

What a man needs in gardening is a cast-iron back, with a hinge in it.

Charles Dudley Warner

In gardens, beauty is a by-product. The main business is sex and death.

Sam Llewellyn

Geriatric Gardening

Then again, if the plant is slow-growing, and you are getting older, you may want to start with a larger plant. I find myself buying larger plants each year.

Bill Cannon

Cherry trees will blossom every year; but I'll disappear for good, one of these days.

Philip Whalen

We come from the earth, we return to the earth, and in between we garden.

Anon

Everything ends with flowers.

Hélène Cixous

If you are not killing plants, you are not really stretching yourself as a gardener.

J. C. Raulston

When gardening, I have one gift you won't find in any manuals. I know it's strange, but I can change perennials to annuals.

Dick Emmons

Old gardeners never die. They just spade away and then throw in the trowel.

Herbert V. Prochnow

I'm not ageing, I just need re-potting.

Anon

Now the gardener is the one who has seen everything ruined so many times that (even as his pain increases with each loss) he comprehends – truly knows – that where there was a garden once, it can be again, or where there never was, there yet can be a garden.

Henry Mitchell

Forty is about the age for unexpected developments: extroverts turn introspective, introverts become sociable, and everyone, without regard to type, acquires grey hairs and philosophies of life. Many also acquire gardens.

Janice Emily Bowens

Mind-Lift

When it comes to staying young, a mind-lift beats a face-lift any day.

Marty Bucella

In my old age there is a coming into flower. My body wanes; mind waxes.

Victor Hugo

Although I am 92, my brain is 30 years old.

Alfred Eisenstaedt

Anyone who stops learning is old, whether at 20 or 80. Anyone who keeps learning stays young. The greatest thing in life is to keep your mind young.

Henry Ford

We get too soon old, and too late smart.

Dutch

Silver Surfers

TECHNOLOGY

—Mother, are you still on the computer?
—Yes, dear. Sometimes you get into a porn loop and just can't get out.

Edina Monsoon and her mother, Absolutely Fabulous

Here I sit, a modern Werther Original. Not telling dusty fairy stories to my from-year-old and feeding him teeth-rotting toffees but teaching him how to work my computer so that one day soon he can teach me things.

Peter Preston

A great way to meet the opposite sex when you're older is on the Internet – a good reason to learn to use a computer. The Internet is 70 per cent men, so the odds are definitely in a woman's favour for finding a guy.

Joan Rivers

My nan said, 'What do you mean when you say the computer went down on you?'

Joseph Longthorne

Experts agree that the best type of computer for your individual needs is one that comes on the market about two days after you actually purchase some other computer.

Dave Barry

During my 87 years, I have witnessed a whole succession of technological revolutions, but none of them has done away with the need for character in the individual, or the ability to think.

Bernard Baruch

Unlike most women of my generation I do love computers, but I get terribly angry when it freezes. You know, it freezes and sends you messages saying you have committed an illegal action. Sorry, I am sitting here minding my own business. I have done nothing wrong. It's you that has frozen. Something has gone wrong in your innards. How dare you blame me?

Sheila Hancock, Grumpy Old Women

How can I believe in God when just last week I got my tongue caught in the roller of an electric typewriter?

Woody Allen

Computers are useless. They can only give you answers.

Pablo Picasso

Television is chewing gum for the eyes.

Frank Lloyd Wright

I am not the only person who uses his computer mainly for the purpose of diddling with his computer.

Dave Barry

It is only when they go wrong that machines remind you how powerful they are.

Clive James

The thing with high-tech is that you always end up using scissors.

David Hockney

I get in a complete rage with the computer. I get all hot, my hair is standing on end, I look like a clown trying to control myself ... Then I get up and walk away and the bloody egg-timer on the screen is still there.

Nina Myskow, Grumpy Old Women

In view of all the deadly computer viruses that have been spreading lately, *Weekend Update* would like to remind you: when you link up to another computer, you're linking up to every computer that that computer has ever linked up to.

Dennis Miller

Technology frightens me to death. It's designed by engineers to impress other engineers, and they always come with instruction booklets that are written by engineers for other engineers – which is why almost no technology ever works.

John Cleese

You switch off and reboot and all this sort of thing. I tell you, I have felt sometimes like opening up the window and hurling my computer out, and the only reason I don't do so is concern for the people down below. Because if you're going to be brained, please not by a computer.

Ann Widdecombe, Grumpy Old Women

Silver Surfers

Oh, they have the Internet on computers now.

Homer Simpson

I hate television. I hate it as much as peanuts. But I can't stop eating peanuts.

Orson Welles

If it weren't for electricity, we'd all be watching television by candlelight.

George Gobel

It was not so long ago that people thought semiconductors were part-time orchestra leaders and microchips were very, very small snack foods.

Geraldine Ferraro

All I need now is a computer. And a 10-year-old kid to teach me how to use it.

Chevy Chase, Fletch Lives

I'm glad cave-people didn't invent television, because they would have just sat around and watched talk shows all day instead of creating tools.

Dave James

I think there is a world market for maybe five computers.

Thomas Watson, Chairman of IBM, 1943

I find television very educating. Every time somebody turns on the set, I go into the other room and read a book.

Groucho Marx

If it weren't for Philo T. Farnsworth, inventor of the television, we'd still be eating frozen radio dinners.

Johnny Carson

Home computers are being called upon to perform many new functions, including the consumption of homework formerly eaten by the dog.

Doug Larson

Her own mother lived the latter years of her life in the horrible suspicion that electricity was dripping invisibly all over the house.

James Thurber

Buying the right computer and getting it to work properly is no more complicated than building a nuclear reactor from wristwatch parts in a darkened room using only your teeth.

Dave Barry

Silver Surfers

I've thrown three mobile phones into the Thames in the past because I couldn't work them. I've never been on the Internet in my life. My wife Barbara gave me a computer but I haven't a clue how to work it.

Rik Mayall

I love technology. Matches, to light a fire, is really high-tech. The wheel is really one of the great inventions of all time. Other than that I am an ignoramus about technology. I once looked for the 'ON' button on the computer and came to find out it was on the back. Then I thought, anyone who would put the 'ON' switch on the back, where you can't find it, doesn't do any good for my psyche. The one time I did get the computer on, I couldn't turn the damn thing off!

William Shatner

I don't care if people think I'm a dumb blonde, or stupid or an average actress or over the hill. I'm gonna have a very successful Internet company and I'm gonna have $100 million in the bank and I don't really give a sh★t what anybody thinks.

Melanie Griffith

A new Viagra virus is going round the Internet. It doesn't affect your hard drive, but you can't minimise anything for hours.

Joan Rivers

Every time you think television has hit its lowest ebb, a new programme comes along to make you wonder where you thought the ebb was.

Art Buchwald

Television is more interesting than people. If it were not we should have people standing in the corner of our room.

Alan Coren

Age and Youth

I am getting older in a country where a major religion is the Church of Acne.

Bill Cosby

When I was young there was no respect for the young, and now that I am old there is no respect for the old. I missed out coming and going.

J.B. Priestley

I'm quite happy about growing older. Who wants to be young? Being 18 is like visiting Russia. You're glad you've had the experience but you'd never want to repeat it.

Barbara Cartland

Age and Youth

When I see a young girl I view her with the same pity that she views me with.

Lilli Palmer

We are happier in many ways when we are old than when we are young. The young sow wild oats, the old grow sage.

Winston Churchill

Young people know the rules. Old people know the exceptions.

Oliver Wendell Holmes

I've got things in my refrigerator older than you.

Lee Trevino to Tiger Woods

Old people have one advantage compared with young ones. They have been young themselves, and young people haven't been old.

Lord Longford

Youth is something very new: 20 years ago no one mentioned it.

Coco Chanel, 1971

There's one thing I have over any 21-year-old: a proud history of accumulated neuroses.

Ray Romano

Age and Youth

Never have I enjoyed youth so thoroughly as I have in my old age.

George Santayana

Young men wish for love, money, and health. One day, they'll say health, money, and love.

Paul Géraldy

Age is not an accomplishment, and youth is not a sin.

Robert Heinlein

This is a youth-orientated society, and the joke is on them because youth is a disease from which we all recover.

Dorothy Fuldheim

All sorts of allowances are made for the illusions of youth, and none for the disenchantments of old age.

Robert Louis Stevenson

I never dared to be radical when young for fear it would make me conservative when old.

Robert Frost

Old age realizes the dreams of youth. Look at Dean Swift: in his youth he built an asylum for the insane; in his old age he was himself an inmate.

Søren Kierkegaard

If youth but knew; if age but could.

Henri Estienne

The belief that youth is the happiest time of life is founded on a fallacy. The happiest person is the person who thinks the most interesting thoughts, and we grow happier as we grow older.

William Phelps

When you are 92 and you say, 'When I was 74,' it's almost like saying, 'When I was young!'

Ernest Waring

Old and young, we are all on our last cruise.

Robert Louis Stevenson

Mind the Gap

THE GENERATION GAP

Blessed are the young for they shall inherit the national debt.

Herbert Hoover

Every generation supposes that the world was simpler for the one before it.

Eleanor Roosevelt

Your modern teenager is not about to listen to advice from an old person, defined as a person who remembers when there was no Velcro.

Dave Barry

I used to call anyone over the age of 35, R. F. C. – Ready For Chrysanthemums.

Brigitte Bardot

My son does not appreciate classical musicians such as the Rolling Stones; he is more into bands with names like 'Heave' and 'Squatting Turnips'.

Dave Barry

The denunciation of the young is a necessary part of the hygiene of older people, and greatly assists the circulation of their blood.

Logan Pearsall Smith

The reason people blame things on the previous generation is that there's only one other choice.

Doug Larson

Parents often talk about the younger generation as if they didn't have anything to do with it.

Haim Ginott

Mind the Gap

There is nothing wrong with the younger generation which the older generation did not outgrow.

Gail Hammond

In case you're worried about what's going to become of the younger generation, it's going to grow up and start worrying about the younger generation.

Roger Allen

One thing only has been lent to youth and age in common: discontent.

Matthew Arnold

The young do not know enough to be prudent, and therefore they attempt the impossible – and achieve it, generation after generation.

Pearl S. Buck

Young men are apt to think themselves wise enough, as drunken men are apt to think themselves sober enough.

Philip Dormer

My generation, faced as it grew with a choice between religious belief and existential despair, chose marijuana. Now we are in our Cabernet stage.

Peggy Noonan

It's not catastrophes, murders, deaths, diseases, that age and kill us; it's the way people look and laugh, and run up the steps of omnibuses.

Virginia Woolf

It's all that the young can do for the old, to shock them and keep them up-to-date.

George Bernard Shaw

Actually, I think children should be taught to be bored. I was in a coma of boredom throughout the 70s. The shops weren't even open on a Sunday, and your nana, both your nanas, came for lunch and you had to be there.

Jenny Eclair, Grumpy Old Women

Methuselah lived to be 969 years old. You boys and girls will see more in the next 50 years than Methuselah saw in his whole lifetime.

Mark Twain

One age blows bubbles and the next breaks them.

William Cowper

But it's hard to be hip over 30 when everyone else is 19, when the last dance we learned was the Lindy, and the last we heard, girls who looked like Barbra Streisand were trying to do something about it.

Judith Viorst

Mind the Gap

When I was as you are now, towering in the confidence of 21, little did I suspect that I should be at 49, what I now am.

Samuel Johnson

My mother is going to have to stop lying about her age because pretty soon I'm going to be older than she is.

Tripp Evans

The question that is so clearly in many potential parents' minds: 'Why should we stunt our ambitions and impoverish our lives in order to be insulted and looked down upon in our old age?'

Joseph A. Schumpeter

But no matter how they make you feel, you should always watch elders carefully. They were you and you will be them. You carry the seeds of your old age in you at this very moment, and they hear the echoes of their childhood each time they see you.

Kent Nerburn

The main thing wrong with the younger generation is that we aren't in it.

Anon

The Good Old Days?

In my old age I find no pleasure save in the memories which I have of the past.

Giacomo Casanova

We have all got our 'good old days' tucked away inside our hearts and we return to them in dreams like cats to favourite armchairs.

Brian Carter

I have liked remembering almost as much as I have liked living.

William Maxwell

Reread all the letters you've kept over the years – the wonderful thing is, you won't have to answer them.

Thora Hird

When we recall the past, we usually find that it is the simplest things – not the great occasions – that in retrospect give off the greatest glory of happiness.

Bob Hope

In July, when I bury my nose in a hazel bush, I feel 15 years old again. It's lovely! It smells of love!

Camille Corot

The Good Old Days?

One of the oddest things in life, I think, is the things one remembers.

Agatha Christie

In memory, everything seems to happen to music.

Tennessee Williams

—Do you remember the minuet?
—Dahling, I can't even remember the men I *slept* with!

Tallulah Bankhead

—During the…
—If you say during the war, I'll pour this cup of tea over your head!
—I wasn't going to say during the war! Bloody little know-all!
—Alright then. Sorry.
—That's alright. During the 1939–1945 conflict with Germany…

Del Boy Trotter and Uncle Albert, Only Fools and Horses

I never saw a banana till I was 14. I was immediately sick after eating it and haven't touched one since.

Enid Bray

In my day, we never got woken up by a Teasmade. We were knocked up every morning by a man with a six-foot pole ... And we weren't having hysterectomies every two minutes, either, like the girls these days. If something went wrong down below, you kept your gob shut and turned up the wireless.

Old Bag, Victoria Wood

I remember when the wireless was something useful. In my day you could warm your hands on the wireless and listen to Terry Wogan. Nowadays all you can do is listen to Wogan.

Paula Brett

In my day, there were things that were done, and things that were not done, and there was even a way of doing things that were not done.

Peter Ustinov

In my day, a juvenile delinquent was a kid who owed tuppence on an overdue library book.

Max Bygraves

My generation thought fast food was something you ate during Lent, a Big Mac was an oversized raincoat and 'crumpet' was something you had for tea. 'Sheltered accommodation' was a place where you waited for a bus, 'time-sharing' meant togetherness and you kept 'coke' in the coal house.

Joan Collins

The Good Old Days?

Went to see *Macbeth*. We walked out in the end. Someone said 'womb'. I said to Col – get your duffle – two pounds on a box of Quality Street and someone says 'womb' … It's happening all over. I mean, in my day, in a magazine, you didn't have sex, you had a row of dots.

Nice Lady, Victoria Wood

When you are about 35 years old, something terrible always happens to music.

Steve Race

At a certain age, you begin to snort at fashion, you stop going to the cinema and you watch the black-and-white classic on aeroplanes. You slouch into a curmudgeonly comfort culture of the old and familiar, and become a 'call that' person. Call that music/fashion/poetry/a chair?

A.A. Gill

Call those pants? I can remember when pants were pants. You wore them for 20 years, then you cut them down for pan scrubs.

Old Bag, Victoria Wood

The Good Old Days?

In my day, men wore driving gloves, women stayed married, and curry had raisins in it.

Swiss Toni, The Fast Show

When I was a child, we took it in turns to have a bath: first the kids, then the whippets, then Granddad.

Ken Dodd

We couldn't afford a proper bath. We just had a pan of water and we'd wash down as far as possible and we'd wash up as far possible. Then, when somebody'd clear the room, we'd wash possible.

Dolly Parton

The older a man gets, the farther he had to walk to school as a boy.

Henry Brightman

In my day, no one had cars. If you wanted to get run over, you'd to catch a bus to the main road … And we didn't do all this keep-fit. We got our exercise lowering coffins out of upstairs windows.

Old Bag, Victoria Wood

Nostalgia is a longing for something you couldn't stand anymore.

Fibber McGee

The Good Old Days?

People say, oh, it's not like the good old days. When were the good old days? In 1900 your doctor was also your barber. 'Say, will you take a little off the sides when you take out my spleen?'

Joe Ditzel

As lousy as things are now, tomorrow they will be somebody's good old days.

Gerald Barzan

If one day you're going to be able to look back on something and laugh about it, you might as well laugh about it now.

Marie Osmond

Always have old memories and young hopes.

Arsene Houssaye

Nothing is more responsible for the good old days than a bad memory.

Franklin P. Adams

When I was young I was called a rugged individualist. When I was in my 50s I was considered eccentric. Here I am doing and saying the same things I did then and I'm labelled senile.

George Burns

We have all passed a lot of water since then.

Samuel Goldwyn

The one thing I remember about Christmas was that my father used to take me out in a boat about 10 miles offshore on Christmas Day, and I used to have to swim back. Extraordinary. It was a ritual. Mind you, that wasn't the hard part. The difficult bit was getting out of the sack.

John Cleese

When you finally go back to your old home town, you find it wasn't the old home you missed but your childhood.

Sam Ewing

The older you get, the more you tell it like it used to be.

Anon

When I was a boy, the Dead Sea was only sick.

George Burns

When I was a kid my parents moved a lot, but I always found them.

Rodney Dangerfield

The Good Old Days?

I was so naive as a kid I used to sneak behind the barn and do nothing.

Johnny Carson

Most people like the old days best – they were younger then.

Anon

I can remember when the air was clean and sex was dirty.

George Burns

There's a lot to do when you're a kid – spiders to catch, girls to poke in the eye – stuff to be getting on with.

Alan Davies

I remember when I was seven, sitting backstage in Vegas while these topless showgirls adjusted their G-strings in front of me. It was a strange way to grow up.

Donny Osmond

Nostalgia, the vice of the aged. We watch so many old movies our memories come in monochrome.

Angela Carter

In every age 'the good old days' were a myth. No one ever thought they were good at the time. For every age has consisted of crises that seemed intolerable to the people who lived through them.

Brooks Atkinson

Nostalgia is a file that removes the rough edges from the good old days.

Doug Larson

We seem to be going through a period of nostalgia, and everyone seems to think yesterday was better than today. I don't think it was, and I would advise you not to wait 10 years before admitting today was great. If you're hung up on nostalgia, pretend today is yesterday and just go out and have one hell of a time.

Art Buchwald

You don't appreciate a lot of stuff in school until you get older. Little things like being spanked every day by a middle-aged woman: stuff you pay good money for in later life.

Emo Philips

Life

Life is a funny thing that happens to you on the way to the grave.

Quentin Crisp

—I go to the market every day to buy a nectarine. At 82, that's life – a round trip on the number 6 bus to buy a nectarine.
—That's so sad.
—Not sad. Life. Sad is when you have to mash the nectarine with a fork.

Sophia Petrillo and Rose Nylund, The Golden Girls

Life is a moderately good play with a badly written third act.

Truman Capote

Life is a marathon in which you reserve the sprint for the end. Mentally I pace myself. I have got an energy bank account and I can't afford to be overdrawn.

Peter Ustinov

Two elderly women are in a restaurant and one of 'em says, 'Boy, the food in this place is really terrible.' The other one says, 'Yeah, I know, and such small portions.' Well, that's essentially how I feel about life. Full of loneliness and misery and suffering … and it's all over much too soon.

Woody Allen

Life can only be understood backwards, but it must be lived forwards.

Søren Kierkegaard

You only live once, but if you do it right, once is enough.

Mae West

Life is rather like opening a tin of sardines. We're all of us looking for the key.

Alan Bennett

What if the hokey cokey really is what it's all about?

Bob Monkhouse

If logic tells you that life is a meaningless accident, don't give up on life. Give up on logic.

Shira Milgrom

The French Marshal Lyautey once asked his gardener to plant a tree. The gardener objected that the tree was slow-growing and would not reach maturity for 100 years. The Marshal replied, 'In that case there is no time to lose. Plant it this afternoon!'

Roland Black

Life

There are only two ways to live your life. One is as though nothing is a miracle. The other is as though everything is a miracle.

Albert Einstein

All life is a failure in the end. The thing is to get sport out of trying.

Sir Francis Chichester

I love living. I have sometimes been wildly, despairingly, acutely miserable, racked with sorrow, but through it all, I still know quite certainly that just to be alive is a grand thing.

Agatha Christie

That it will never come again is what makes life so sweet.

Emily Dickinson

The answer to old age is to keep one's mind busy and to go on with one's life as if it were interminable. I always admired Chekhov for building a new house when he was dying of tuberculosis.

Leon Edel

I believe you should live each day as if it was your last, which is why I don't have any clean laundry, because who wants to wash clothes on the last day of their life?

Jack Handey

With whitened hair, desires failing, strength ebbing out of him, with the sun gone down and with only the serenity and the calm warning of the evening star left to him, he drank to Life, to all it had been, to what it was, to what it would be. Hurrah!

Sean O'Casey

Experience

Experience is the one thing you have plenty of when you're too old to get the job.

Laurence J. Peter

Experience is the name everyone gives to their mistakes.

Oscar Wilde

Experience is a comb life gives you after you lose your hair.

Judith Stern

A prune is an experienced plum.

John Trattner

I have learned throughout my life as a composer chiefly through my mistakes and pursuits of false assumptions, not by my exposure to wisdom and founts of knowledge.

Igor Stravinsky

We learn from experience that man never learns from experience.

George Bernard Shaw

If we could sell our experiences for what they cost us, we'd all be millionaires.

Abigail Van Buren

Sagacity

WISDOM

And in the end, it's not the years in your life that count. It's the life in your years.

Abraham Lincoln

All would live long, but none would be old.

Benjamin Franklin

There are compensations for growing older. One is the realisation that to be sporting isn't at all necessary. It is a great relief to reach this stage of wisdom.

Cornelius Otis Skinner

Despite my 30 years of research into the feminine soul, I have not yet been able to answer the great question that has never been answered: What does a woman want?

Sigmund Freud

No man loves life like him that's growing old.

Sophocles

Old age deprives the intelligent man only of qualities useless to wisdom.

Joseph Joubert

If a human is modest and satisfied, old age will not be heavy on him. If he is not, even youth will be a burden.

Plato

The older I grow, the more I listen to people who don't say much.

Germain G. Glidden

Sagacity

The more sand that has escaped from the hourglass of our life, the clearer we should see through it.

Anon

The man who views the world at 50 the same as he did at 20 has wasted 30 years of his life.

Muhammad Ali

Early to rise and early to bed. Makes a male healthy, wealthy and dead.

James Thurber

If you wait, all that happens is that you get older.

Mario Andretti

Everyone should keep a mental wastepaper basket and the older he grows the more things he will consign to it – torn up to irrecoverable tatters.

Samuel Butler

The thing you realise as you get older is that parents don't know what the hell they're doing and neither will you when you get to be a parent.

Mark Hoppus

As you get older, though, you realise there are fire extinguishers. You do have an ability to control the flames.

Chaka Khan

And you learn as you get older, you learn to play the pauses better.

Michael Parkinson

The older we grow, the greater becomes our wonder at how much ignorance one can contain without bursting one's clothes.

Mark Twain

You can tell a lot about a fellow's character by his way of eating jellybeans.

Ronald Reagan

I'm very pleased with each advancing year. It stems back to when I was 40. I was a bit upset about reaching that milestone, but an older friend consoled me. 'Don't complain about growing old – many, many people do not have that privilege.'

Earl Warren

Many are saved from sin by being so inept at it.

Mignon McLaughlin

Sagacity

Life's under no obligation to give us what we expect.

Margaret Mitchell

You can't be brave if you've only had wonderful things happen to you.

Mary Tyler Moore

Wisdom doesn't necessarily come with age.
Sometimes age just shows up all by itself.

Tom Wilson

Old age comes at a bad time.

San Banducci

We all take different paths in life, but no matter where we go, we take a little of each other everywhere.

Tim McGraw

Perhaps one has to be very old before one learns to be amused rather than shocked.

Pearl S. Buck

It takes about 10 years to get used to how old you are.

Anon

In three words I can sum up everything I've learned about life: it goes on.

Robert Frost

My father always used to say that when you die, if you've got five real friends, then you've had a great life.

Lee Iacocca

You see things, and you say, 'Why?' But I dream things that never were, and I say, 'Why not?'

George Bernard Shaw

Old age is life's parody.

Simone de Beauvoir

The end comes when we no longer talk with ourselves. It is the end of genuine thinking and the beginning of the final loneliness.

Eric Hoffer

Minds ripen at very different ages.

Elizabeth Montagu

To be 70 years young is sometimes far more cheerful and hopeful than to be 40 years old.

Oliver Wendell Holmes Jr.

Sagacity

The old believe everything;
The middle-aged suspect everything;
The young know everything.

Oscar Wilde

He who laughs most, learns best.

John Cleese

Wherever there is power, there is age. Don't be deceived by dimples and curls. I tell you that babe is a thousand years old.

Ralph Waldo Emerson

Error is acceptable as long as we are young; but one must not drag it along into old age.

Johann Wolfgang von Goethe

Adulthood is the ever-shrinking period between childhood and old age. It is the apparent aim of modern industrial societies to reduce this period to a minimum.

Thomas Szasz

Many talents preserve their precociousness right into old age.

Karl Kraus

All the world's a stage and most of us are desperately unrehearsed.

Sean O'Casey

What do I know of man's destiny? I could tell you more about radishes.

Samuel Beckett

Few people think more than two or three times a year; I have made an international reputation for myself by thinking once or twice a week.

George Bernard Shaw

If at first you don't succeed, failure may be your style.

Quentin Crisp

Honest criticism is hard to take, particularly from a relative, a friend, an acquaintance or a stranger.

Franklin P. Jones

Seventy per cent of success in life is showing up.

Woody Allen

If you can't convince them, confuse them.

Harry S. Truman

Sagacity

A positive attitude may not solve all your problems, but it will annoy enough people to make it worth the effort.

Herm Albright

Misers aren't much fun to live with, but they do make wonderful ancestors.

Anon

Past is past and we must live the present to survive the future.

Martin Ducavne

The future is assured. It's just the past that keeps changing.

Russian joke

May the best of your past be the worst of your future.

Anon

The past is history; the future is a mystery; this moment is a gift; that is why this moment is called the present; enjoy it.

Allan Johnson

Know what's weird? Day by day, nothing seems to change, but pretty soon … everything's different.

Calvin, Calvin and Hobbes

Imagination was given to man to compensate him for what he isn't. A sense of humour was provided to console him for what he is.

Horace Walpole

You were born an original. Don't die a copy.

John Mason

To be able to feel the lightest touch really is a gift.

Christopher Reeve

If women ran the world we wouldn't have wars, just intense negotiations every 28 days.

Robin Williams

If you think before you speak the other guy gets his joke in first.

Jimmy Nail

For a happy and successful life you need a love of people and a love of maths.

Johnny Ball

If you obey all the rules, you miss all the fun.

Katharine Hepburn

People always call it luck when you've acted more sensibly than they have.

Anne Tyler

You don't stop laughing when you grow old; you grow old when you stop laughing.

Anon

Good and Bad

Old age is a great trial. One has to be so damned *good*!

May Sarton

When you are younger you get blamed for crimes you never committed and when you're older you begin to get credit for virtues you never possessed. It evens itself out.

I.F. Stone

Basil Blackwell said that he had certainly been depraved by the book *Last Exit to Brooklyn*, but as he was in his 80s at the time the matter didn't seem to be of great practical significance.

John Mortimer

What on earth has happened to outrage? There is a hell of a lot in this life to be furious about – and not just things affecting older people – and yet everybody seems to be taking it all so easy. We want more outrage.

Margaret Simey

Old age is an excellent time for outrage. My goal is to say or do at least one outrageous thing every week.

Maggie Kuhn

An 80-year-old man sentenced to 10 years in jail, said to the judge, 'I'll never live that long.' The judge replied, 'Well, do the best you can.'

Anon

Years and sins are always more than acknowledged.

Italian proverb

One should never make one's debut with a scandal; one should reserve that to give interest in one's old age.

Oscar Wilde

Old men like giving good advice to console themselves for no longer being able to set bad examples.

La Rochefoucauld

Don't worry about avoiding temptation – as you grow older, it starts avoiding you.

Michael Ford

Thank You for Being a Friend

FRIENDSHIP

As life goes on, don't you find that all you need is about two real friends, a regular supply of books, and a Peke?

P. G. Wodehouse

We need old friends to help us grow old and new friends to help us stay young.

Letty Cottin Pogrebin

One consolation of ageing is realizing that while you have been growing old your friends haven't been standing still in the matter, either.

Clare Boothe Luce

The mere process of growing old together will make our slightest acquaintances seem like bosom-friends.

Logan Pearsall Smith

When you're 50 you start thinking about things you haven't thought about before. I used to think getting old was about vanity – but actually it's about losing people you love. Getting wrinkles is trivial.

Joyce Carol Oates

If I had any decency, I'd be dead. Most of my friends are.

Dorothy Parker

The loss of friends is a tax on age!

Ninon de Lenclos

I don't have a warm personal enemy left. They've all died off. I miss them terribly because they helped define me.

Clare Boothe Luce

My only profile of heaven is a large blue sky … larger than the biggest I have seen in June – and in it are my friends – every one of them.

Emily Dickinson

All my friends are dead. They're all in heaven now and they're all up there mingling with one another. By now, they are starting to wonder if I might have gone to the other place.

Teresa Platt

Going, Going, Gone!

DEATH

Like everyone else who makes the mistake of getting older, I begin each day with coffee and obituaries.

Bill Cosby

I get up each morning and dust off my wits,
Pick up the paper and read the obits.
If my name isn't there I know I'm not dead;
I have a good breakfast and go back to bed.

Anon

Why did I not do more in my life, I ask myself, as I read the obituaries of the people who have crammed their lives with 'doing' while I have wasted great chunks of mine dreaming?

Mary Wesley

My old mam read the obituary column every day but she could never understand how people always die in alphabetical order.

Frank Carson

I have never killed a man, but I have read many obituaries with great pleasure.

Clarence Darrow

When I get in a taxi, the first thing they say is, 'Hello Eric, I thought you were dead.'

Eric Sykes

I have been dead for two years, but I don't choose to have it known.

Lord Chesterfield

There are so many ways of dying, it is astonishing that any of us choose old age.

Beryl Bainbridge

There are worse things to die of than old age.

Clive James

How young can you die of old age?

Steven Wright

Hope I die before I get old.

Pete Townshend

I want to die young at an advanced age.

Max Lerner

Statistics tell us that Audrey Hepburn died young. What no statistics can show us is that she would have died young at any age.

Peter Ustinov

Going, Going, Gone!

Jesus died too soon. If he had lived to my age he would have repudiated his doctrine.

Friedrich Nietzsche, 48

I don't mind dying. Trouble is, you feel so bloody stiff the next day.

George Axelrod

It seems like the only two times they pronounce you anything in life is when they pronounce you 'man and wife' or 'dead on arrival'.

Dennis Miller

—When we die, certain things keep growing – your fingernails, the hair on your head, the hair on your chest…
—Not the hair on *my* chest!
—My dear, you give up hope too easily.

Lawrence Olivier and Edith Evans

For three days after death, hair and fingernails continue to grow but phone calls taper off.

Johnny Carson

Better take my photograph now, dear – I'm 80, I might die at lunch.

Lady Diana Cooper to a magazine photographer

At a formal dinner party, the person nearest death should always be seated closest to the bathroom.

George Carlin

I am ready to meet my Maker. Whether my Maker is ready for the ordeal of meeting me is another matter.

Winston Churchill, on his 75th birthday

My family has a propensity – it must be in our genes – for dropping dead. Here one minute, gone the next. Neat. I pray that I have inherited this gene.

Mary Wesley

—How would you like to die?
—At the end of a sentence.

Interviewer and Peter Ustinov

My dream is to die in a tub of ice cream, with Mel Gibson.

Joan Rivers

Let me die eating ortolans to the sound of soft music.

Benjamin Disraeli

I shall not die of a cold. I shall die of having lived.

Willa Cather

Going, Going, Gone!

Errol Flynn died on a 70-foot yacht with a 17-year-old girl. My husband's always wanted to go that way, but he's going to settle for a 17-footer and a 70-year-old.

Mrs Walter Cronkite

—I've decided I want to be cremated.
—C'mon then, Nana, get your coat…

Alfie and Nana Moon, EastEnders

Where would I like my ashes scattered? I don't know. Surprise me.

Bob Hope

I told my wife I want to be cremated. She's planning a barbecue.

Rodney Dangerfield

I've never fancied being cremated or buried. I keep hoping I can hold out long enough for someone to discover some new and more suitable medium for my expiry. Evaporation through abstruse sentence, say. Interment in metaphor. Scatter me in words, O my beloved.

Howard Jacobson

If there wasn't death, I think you couldn't go on.

Stevie Smith

It was Death – possibly the only dinner guest more unwelcome than Sidney Poitier.

Kinky Friedman

Death is nature's way of saying, 'Your table is ready.'

Robin Williams

Dying is a very dull, dreary affair. And my advice to you is to have nothing whatever to do with it.

Somerset Maugham

I'm not afraid to die, honey. In fact I'm kinda looking forward to it. I know that the Lord has his arms wrapped around this big, fat sparrow.

Ethel Waters

I'm not afraid of death. It's the stake one puts up in order to play the game of life.

Jean Giraudoux

It's not that I'm afraid to die. I just don't want to be there when it happens.

Woody Allen

Going, Going, Gone!

Dying is no big deal. The least of us will manage that. Living is the trick. My life has been strawberries in the wintertime, and you can't ask for more than that.

Red Smith

Perhaps passing through the gates of death is like passing quietly through the gate in a pasture fence. On the other side, you keep walking, without the need to look back. No shock, no drama, just the lifting of a plank or two in a simple wooden gate in a clearing. Neither pain, nor floods of light, not great voices, but just the silent crossing of a meadow.

Mark Helperin

What a simple thing death is, just as simple as the falling of an autumn leaf.

Vincent Van Gogh

Under the soil, I'll become part of a daisy or a cowslip. To return to the earth will be a kind of reincarnation.

Joan Bakewell

Life is a great surprise. I do not see why death should not be an even greater one.

Vladimir Nabokov

At my age, I'm often asked if I'm frightened of death and my reply is always, I can't remember being frightened of birth.

Peter Ustinov

To die will be an awfully big adventure.

J. M. Barrie

Dying is one of the few things that can be done just as easily lying down.

Woody Allen

I'm dying but otherwise I'm in very good health.

Edith Sitwell

Life is too short but it would be absolutely awful if it were too long.

Peter Ustinov

Death in life; death without its privileges, death without its benefits. Who would want that? If you find you can't make 70 by any but an uncomfortable road, don't you go. When they take off the Pullman and retire you to the rancid smoker, put on your things, count your cheques, and get out at the first way station where there's a cemetery.

Mark Twain

Going, Going, Gone!

I have always admired Esquimaux. One fine day a delicious meal is cooked for dear old mother, and then she goes walking away over the ice, and doesn't come back … One should be proud of leaving life like that – with dignity and resolution.

Agatha Christie

We should be more like elephants. When they are dying they creep off and get out of the way.

Mary Warnock, 80

Like a prisoner awaiting his release, like a schoolboy when the end of term is near, like a migrant bird ready to fly south … I long to be gone.

Malcolm Muggeridge

—When my time comes, I sure want somebody to put me out of my misery if something tragic happens, like I get a fatal illness or I've lost my looks.
—Just tell us when, Blanche.

Blanche Devereaux and Dorothy Zbornak, The Golden Girls

If I'm ever stuck on a respirator or a life support system I definitely want to be unplugged. But not until I'm down to a size 8.

Henriette Mantel

Euthanasia is a way of putting old people out of their family's misery.

Mike Barfield

My husband died aged 79. He led a wonderful life and never suffered unless I wanted him to.

Suzanne Sugarbaker, Women of the House

My husband died while we were making love. I thought it was funny when he kept saying, 'I'm going! ... I'm going!'

Rose Nylund, The Golden Girls

On Sunday 5 April 1998, following a courageous fight for life, Catherine Thomas (née Holder) surrounded by family, died at home – and she's bloody annoyed.

Obituary notice, Cardiff newspaper

When I told my daughter that Edith Evans had died, she said, 'I don't believe it. She's not the type.'

Bryan Forbes

George Gershwin died on 11 July 1937, but I don't have to believe it if I don't want to.

John O'Hara

Going, Going, Gone!

There is something about a poet which leads us to believe that he died, in many cases, as long as 20 years before his birth.

James Thurber

The man who invented the hokey cokey has died. His funeral was a strange affair. First, they put his left leg in…

Al Ferrera

Martin Levine has passed away at the age of 75. Mr Levine had owned a movie-theatre chain in New York. The funeral will be held on Thursday at 2.15, 4.20, 6.30, 8.40, and 10.50.

David Letterman

The inventor of Crest passed away. Four out of five dentists came to the funeral.

Jay Leno

Funeral services were held this week for 82-year-old chewing-gum magnate Philip K. Wrigley. In keeping with his last request, Wrigley's remains will be stuck to the bottom of a luncheonette counter.

Jane Curtin

The chairman of MORI polls has died. He'll be missed by 80 per cent of his family and 35 per cent of his friends.

Craig Kilborn

The Lucky Stiff Funeral Home: We Put the Fun into Funeral.

The Simpsons

They say such lovely things about people at their funerals. It's a shame I'm going to miss mine by just a few days.

Bob Monkhouse

Why is it that we rejoice at a birth and grieve at a funeral? Is it because we are not the person involved?

Mark Twain

This is the last time I will take part as an amateur.

Daniel François Esprit Auber, 76, at a funeral

There's nothing like a morning funeral for sharpening the appetite for lunch.

Arthur Marshall

Going, Going, Gone!

I always thought I'd be the first to go … Weren't they lovely, them vol au vent. What was in 'em? It was a sort of mushroomy thing. Hey, can I have them when I go, Barbara?

Nana, The Royle Family

I used to hate weddings – all those old dears poking me in the stomach and saying, 'You're next.' But they stopped all that when I started doing the same to them at funerals.

Gail Flynn

In Liverpool, the difference between a funeral and a wedding is one less drunk.

Paul O'Grady

When you're my age, you worry about two things. One is when a woman says, 'Let's do it again, right now,' and the other is, 'Who's going to come to my funeral?'

Alan King

Always go to other people's funerals, otherwise they won't come to yours.

Yogi Berra

No matter how rich you become, how famous or powerful, when you die the size of your funeral will still pretty much depend on the weather.

Michael Pritchard

In the city a funeral is just an interruption in the traffic; in the country it is a form of popular entertainment.

George Ade

A stooped old man stood, deep in thought, watching the funeral procession pass by. I whispered to him, 'Who died?' He said, 'The one in the first car.'

Seamus Flynn

Memorial services are the cocktail parties of the geriatric set.

John Gielgud

The trouble with quotes about death is that 99.99 per cent of them are made by people who are still alive.

Joshua Burns

I don't want to achieve immortality through my work, I want to achieve it through not dying.

Woody Allen

Going, Going, Gone!

There are three natural anaesthetics: sleep, fainting, and death.

Oliver Wendell Holmes

Tears are sometimes an inappropriate response to death. When a life has been lived completely honestly, completely successfully, or just completely, the correct response to death's perfect punctuation mark is a smile.

Julie Burchill

Death is just nature's way of telling you to slow down.

Dick Sharples

The fear of death is the most unjustified of all fears, for there's no risk of accident for someone who's dead.

Albert Einstein

Death is the greatest kick of all – that's why they save it till last.

Graffito

The closing years of life are like the end of a masquerade party, when the masks are dropped.

Arthur Schopenhauer

The world is getting to be such a dangerous place, a guy is lucky to get out of it alive.

W. C. Fields

What's death like? It's as bad as the chicken at Tresky's Restaurant.

Woody Allen

When I die, I want it to be on my hundredth birthday, in my beach house on Maui, and I want my husband to be so upset he has to drop out of college.

Roz Doyle, Frasier

Life is pleasant. Death is peaceful.
It's the transition that's troublesome.

Isaac Asimov

I'd rather be dead than singing 'Satisfaction' when I'm 45.

Mick Jagger

I enjoy life. I think I'll enjoy death even more.

Cat Stevens

I wanted to be bored to death – as good a way to go as any.

Peter De Vries

Going, Going, Gone!

One thing about being successful is that I stopped being afraid of dying. Once you're a star you're dead already. You're embalmed.

Dustin Hoffman

The report of my death was an exaggeration.

Mark Twain

I'd hate to die twice. It's so boring.

Richard P. Feynman

Dying is easy. Comedy is difficult.

Edmund Gwenn

The idea is to die young as late as possible.

Ashley Montagu

It's funny how most people love the dead, once you're dead you're made for life.

Jimi Hendrix

I fear vastly more a futile, incompetent old age than I do any form of death.

William Allen White

I don't believe in dying. It's been done. I'm working on a new exit.

George Burns

Everyone is afraid of dying alone. I don't understand. Who wants to die and have to be polite at the same time?

Quentin Crisp

The first sign of his approaching end was when one of my old aunts, when undressing him, removed a toe with one of his socks.

Graham Greene

Death will be a great relief. No more interviews.

Katharine Hepburn

Everybody has got to die but I have always believed an exception would be made in my case.

William Saroyan

First thing I do when I wake up in the morning is breathe on the mirror and hope it fogs.

Earl Wynn

I can't die. It would ruin my image.

Jack LaLanne

Going, Going, Gone!

If you die in an elevator, be sure to push the up button.

Sam Levenson

My father passed away very quietly in his sleep – between the bar and the gents.

Barry Humphries

Death is a low chemical trick played on everybody except sequoia trees.

J. J. Furnas

I'm not afraid of death. It's the makeover at the undertaker's that scares me ... They try to make you look as lifelike as possible, which defeats the whole purpose. It's hard to feel bad for somebody who looks better than you do.

Anita Wise

The difference between sex and death is that with death you can do it alone and no one is going to make fun of you.

Woody Allen

Eternity is a terrible thought. I mean, where's it going to end?

Tom Stoppard

If I could drop dead right now, I'd be the happiest man alive.

Samuel Goldwyn

The only completely consistent people are the dead.

Aldous Huxley

I don't think kids have a problem with death. It's us older ones who are nearer to it that start being frightened.

Helena Bonham Carter

Don't be afraid your life will end; be afraid that it will never begin.

Grace Hansen

Dying doesn't frighten me in the slightest though I should love to see my grandchildren grow up, but I don't want to get old and infirm and not be able to enjoy my life.

Beryl Bainbridge

I know a woman who had her husband cremated and then mixed his ashes with grass and smoked him. She said it was the best he'd made her feel in years.

Maureen Murphy

Going, Going, Gone!

Once the game is over, the king and the pawn go back in the same box.

Italian proverb

I'm the one that's got to die when it's time for me to die, so let me live my life the way I want to.

Jimi Hendrix

He who dies with the most toys is, nonetheless, still dead.

Anon

Either he's dead or my watch has stopped.

Groucho Marx

It's impossible to experience one's death objectively and still carry a tune.

Woody Allen

In the end, everything is a gag.

Charlie Chaplin

To lose one parent may be regarded as a misfortune; to lose both looks like carelessness.

Oscar Wilde

I wouldn't mind dying – it's the business of having to stay dead that scares the sh*t out of me.

R. Geis

With the newspaper strike on, I wouldn't consider dying.

Bette Davis, on being told that her death was rumoured

Death would be a beautiful place if it looks like Brad Pitt.

Carmen Electra

When it comes time to die, be not like those whose hearts are filled with the fear of death, so when their time comes they weep and pray for a little more time to live their lives over again in a different way. Sing your death song, and die like a hero going home.

Mohican Chief Aupumut

If my doctor told me I had only six minutes to live, I wouldn't brood. I'd type a little faster.

Isaac Asimov

When I die I want to decompose in a barrel of porter and have it served in all the pubs in Ireland.

J. P. Donleavy, The Ginger Man

Going, Going, Gone!

My young son asked me what happens after we die. I told him we get buried under a bunch of dirt and worms eat our bodies. I guess I should have told him the truth – that most of us go to Hell and burn eternally – but I didn't want to upset him.

Jack Handey

Every man of genius is considerably helped by being dead.

Robert Lynd

Alas, I am dying beyond my means.

Oscar Wilde

My grandmother made dying her life's work.

Hugh Leonard

I would never die for my beliefs because I might be wrong.

Bertrand Russell

Sure there have been injuries and deaths in boxing – but none of them serious.

Alan Minter

There's something about death that is comforting. The thought that you could die tomorrow frees you to appreciate your life now.

Angelina Jolie

Life does not cease to be funny when people die any more than it ceases to be serious when people laugh.

George Bernard Shaw

When I die, just keep playing the records.

Jimi Hendrix

Excuse My Dust

EPITAPH

Didn't wake up this morning.

Epitaph for a blues singer

Did you hear about my operation?

Warner Baxter

I told you I was sick.

Spike Milligan

Let's do lunch next week.

Raoul Lionel Felder

Excuse My Dust

Stiff at last.

Anon

By and by, God caught his eye.

George S. Kaufman, epitaph for a waiter

Surrounded by fucking idiots.

Lindsay Anderson

My uncle Sammy was an angry man. He had printed on his tombstone: What are you looking at?

Margaret Smith

A damn good funeral is still one of our best and cheapest acts of theatre.

Gwyn Thomas

My luck is so bad that if I bought a cemetery, people would stop dying.

Ed Furgol

When I have one foot in the grave, I will tell the whole truth about women. I shall tell it, jump into my coffin, pull the lid over me and say, 'Do what you like now.'

Leo Tolstoy

My grandfather was a very insignificant man, actually. At his funeral his hearse followed the other cars.

Woody Allen

Here lies the body of Mary Ann Lowder.
She burst while drinking a seltzer powder.
Called from the world to her heavenly rest,
She should have waited till it effervesced.

Anon

In India when a man dies, his widow throws herself on the funeral pyre. Over here, she says, 'Fifty ham baps, Beryl – you slice, I'll butter.'

Victoria Wood

There's no such thing as bad publicity except your own obituary.

Brendan Behan

When I am dead, I hope it may be said: 'His sins were scarlet but his books were read.'

Hilaire Belloc

Here lies Jan Smith, wife of Thomas Smith, Marble Cutter. This monument was erected by her husband as a tribute to her memory and a specimen of his work. Monuments of this same style are $250.

Gravestone inscription

Excuse My Dust

Son: Do you want to be buried, Mum? Or shall we have you cremated?
Mother: Oh, I don't know, love. Surprise me!

Deric Longden

Edina: No, no, no grave for me, sweetie. I'm a Buddhist anyway. I want to be lain out on a rock in the middle of the Ganges, darling, and then just pecked by birds. I don't want to end up as some drugged-up zombie in a hospital, all right?
Saffie: I thought that would appeal to you…

Absolutely Fabulous

This is on me.

Dorothy Parker, suggestion for her tombstone

She did it the hard way.

Bette Davis's epitaph

Called back.

Emily Dickinson's epitaph

Here lies W. C. Fields. I would rather be living in Philadelphia.

W. C. Fields's suggestion for his epitaph to Vanity Fair *in 1925*

I always remember an epitaph which is in the cemetery at Tombstone, Arizona. It says: 'Here lies Jack Williams. He done his damnedest.' I think that is the greatest epitaph a man can have.

Harry S. Truman

Over my dead body!

George S. Kaufman, suggested epitaph

A funeral eulogy is a belated plea for the defence delivered after the evidence is all in.

Irvin S. Cobb

When I die, my epitaph should read: She Paid the Bills. That's the story of my private life.

Gloria Swanson

May my husband rest in peace till I get there.

Dame Edna Everage

Everybody loves you when you're six foot in the ground.

John Lennon

I was terrible at straight items. When I wrote obituaries, my mother said the only thing I ever got them to do was die in alphabetical order.

Erma Bombeck

When you've told someone that you've left them a legacy the only decent thing to do is to die at once.

Samuel Butler

I wish to be cremated. One-tenth of my ashes shall be given to my agent, as written in our contract.

Groucho Marx

Never say you know a person until you have divided an inheritance with them.

Johann Lavater

Famous Last Words

Bless you, Sister. May all your sons be bishops.

Brendan Behan

Why not? After all, it belongs to him.

Charlie Chaplin, after a priest said, 'May the Lord have mercy on your soul.'

Never felt better.

Douglas Fairbanks Snr.

That was a great game of golf, fellers.

Harry Lillis 'Bing' Crosby

God damn the whole friggin' world but you, Carlotta.

W. C. Fields

On the contrary.

Henrik Ibsen, after hearing a nurse remark that he was feeling better

This is it! I'm going. I'm going.

Al Jolson

Bugger Bognor.

George V, having been assured by his physician that he would soon be fit enough to holiday in Bognor Regis

Why not? Yeah. Beautiful.

Timothy Leary

Is everybody happy? I want everybody to be happy. I know I'm happy.

Ethel Barrymore

Go on, get out! Last words are for fools who haven't said enough!

Karl Marx

Why should I talk to you? I've just been talking to your boss.

Wilson Mizner, to a priest standing over his bed

Famous Last Words

Born in a hotel room and, goddamn it, died in a hotel room.

Eugene O'Neill

Drink to me!

Pablo Picasso

God bless … God damn.

James Thurber

Go away. I'm all right.

H. G. Wells

Curtain! Fast music! Lights! Ready for the last finale! Great! The show looks good. The show looks good.

Florenz Ziegfeld, Broadway producer

Die? I should say not, dear fellow. No Barrymore would allow such a conventional thing to happen to him.

John Barrymore

Friends, applaud: the comedy is finished.

Ludwig van Beethoven

I am about to – or I am going to – die: either expression is correct.

Dominique Bouhours, French grammarian

Goodnight, my darlings, I'll see you tomorrow.

Noël Coward

Why do you weep? Did you think I was immortal?

Louis XIV, King of France

Sister, you're trying to keep me alive as an old curiosity, but I'm done, I'm finished, I'm going to die.

George Bernard Shaw, to his nurse

Oh, I am not going to die, am I? He will not separate us, we have been so happy.

Charlotte Brontë, to her husband of nine months, Rev. Arthur Nicholls

I've had 18 straight whiskies, I think that's the record...

Dylan Thomas

I should never have switched from Scotch to Martinis.

Humphrey Bogart

I've had a hell of a lot of fun and I've enjoyed every minute of it.

Errol Flynn

Famous Last Words

I have offended God and mankind because my work did not reach the quality it should have.

Leonardo da Vinci

My wallpaper and I are fighting a duel to the death. One or the other of us has to go.

Oscar Wilde

This isn't *Hamlet*, you know, it's not meant to go into the bloody ear.

Laurence Olivier, to his nurse, who had spilt water on him

Dammit … Don't you dare ask God to help me.

Joan Crawford, after her housekeeper began to pray aloud

This is absurd!

Sigmund Freud

I'd rather be skiing than doing what I'm doing.

Stan Laurel

It's all been rather lovely.

John Le Mesurier

Die, my dear doctor? That's the last thing I shall do.

Lord Palmerston

If this is dying, I don't think much of it.

Lytton Strachey

I'll always remember the last words of my grandfather, 'A truck!'

Emo Philips

Afterlife and Immortality

Death is not the end. There remains the litigation over the estate.

Ambrose Bierce

I owe much; I have nothing; the rest I leave to the poor.

François Rabelais

Almost everyone, when age, disease or sorrows strike him, inclines to think there is a God, or something very like Him.

Arthur Hugh Clough

I do benefits for all religions. I'd hate to blow the hereafter on a technicality.

Bob Hope

Afterlife and Immortality

Life after death is as improbable as sex after marriage.

Madeleine Kahn, Clue

When I approach the pearly gates, I'd like to hear a Champagne cork popping, an orchestra tuning up, and the sound of my mother laughing.

Patricia Routledge

Billy Graham described heaven as a family reunion that never ends. What could hell possibly be like? Home videos of the same reunion?

Dennis Miller

After your death you will be what you were before your birth.

Arthur Schopenhauer

I intend to live forever. So far, so good.

Steven Wright

Millions long for immortality who do not know what to do with themselves on a rainy Sunday afternoon.

Susan Ertz

If we were promised eternal life we would shriek for the promise of death.

A. A. Gardiner

Afterlife and Immortality

If I have any beliefs about immortality, it is that certain dogs I have known will go to heaven, and very, very few persons.

James Thurber

Ah, well, there is just this world and then the next, and then all our troubles will be over with.

Margot Asquith

I don't believe in an afterlife, although I am bringing a change of underwear.

Woody Allen

Everybody wants to go to Heaven, but nobody wants to die.

Joe Louis

In Heaven all the interesting people are missing.

Friedrich Nietzsche

The Devil himself had probably redesigned Hell in the light of information he had gained from observing airport layouts.

Anthony Price

...to be in a crowded theatre with lots of old people is quite frightening. Surrounded by men in tartan trousers and bifocals and women whose last orgasm coincided with the Suez crises, it was like being in the waiting room for heaven.

Gareth McLean

When did I realise I was God? Well, I was praying and I suddenly realised I was talking to myself.

Peter O'Toole

And God said, 'Let there be light' and there was light, but the Electricity Board said He would have to wait until Thursday to be connected.

Spike Milligan

Maybe there is no actual place called Hell. Maybe Hell is just having to listen to our grandparents breathe through their noses when they're eating sandwiches.

Jim Carrey

If you're going through Hell, keep going.

Sir Winston Churchill

What! You been keeping records on me? I wasn't so bad! How many times did I take the Lord's name in vain? One million and six! Jesus Ch...!

Steve Martin

Afterlife and Immortality

I can't stand light. I hate weather. My idea of Heaven is moving from one smoke-filled room to another.

Peter O'Toole

When we drink, we get drunk. When we get drunk, we fall asleep. When we fall asleep, we commit no sin. When we commit no sin, we go to Heaven. So, let's all get drunk and go to Heaven!

Brian O'Rourke

When I die, I hope to go to Heaven, whatever the Hell that is.

Ayn Rand

There is no Hell. There is only France.

Frank Zappa

What a pity Hell's gates are not kept by O'Flynn
The surly old dog would let nobody in.

Patrick Ireland, on the epitaph of an Irish security guard

God is love. I have loved. Therefore, I will go to heaven.

Imelda Marcos

Hell is full of musical amateurs.

George Bernard Shaw

Wisdom and Advice

—Old Timer, I have journeyed far to seek the benefit of your immense knowledge and wisdom acquired over a long lifetime. Do you have any words to share?
—Nope.

Richie Ryan and Methos, Highlander

Wisdom doesn't always show up with age. Sometimes age shows up all by itself.

Tom Wilson

When I was young, I was told: 'You'll see, when you're 50.' I'm 50 and I haven't seen a thing.

Erik Satie

From the earliest times the old have rubbed it into the young that they are wiser than they, and before the young had discovered what nonsense this was they were old, too, and it profited them to carry on the imposture.

Somerset Maugham

I was telling my son about the advantages of being over 50. 'As you get older,' I explained, 'you get wiser.' He just looked at me and said, 'In that case you must be a genius.'

Angus Walker

I gave my beauty and my youth to men. I am going to give my wisdom and experience to animals.

Brigitte Bardot

To my extreme mortification, I grow wiser every day.

Lady Mary Wortley Montagu

By the time you're 80 years old you've learned everything. You only have to remember it.

George Burns

Think, man, think … what would Thora Hird do?

Brian Potter, Phoenix Nights

Whenever I'm confused, I just check my underwear. It holds the answer to all the important questions.

Grampa Simpson, The Simpsons

I have studied many philosophers and many cats. The wisdom of cats is infinitely superior.

Hippolyte Taine

Since I got to 80, I've started reading the Bible a lot more. It's kind of like cramming for my finals.

Vincent Watson

Wisdom and Advice

The whiter my hair becomes, the more ready people are to believe what I say.

Bertrand Russell

Grandfather is the wisest person in the house but few of the household listen.

Chinese proverb

Ask the opinion of an older one and a younger than thyself, and return to thine own opinion.

Egyptian proverb

Trust one who has gone through it.

Virgil

I've been things and seen places.

Mae West

I wish I didn't know now what I didn't know then.

Bob Seger

It is time, at 56, to begin, at least, to know oneself – and I do know what I am not.

John Constable

We should be careful to get out of an experience only the wisdom that is in it – and stop there; lest we be like the cat that sits down on a hot stove-lid. She will never sit down on a hot stove-lid again – and that is well; but also she will never sit down on a cold one any more.

Mark Twain

If age imparted wisdom, there wouldn't be any old fools.

Claudia Young

Sometimes one likes foolish people for their folly, better than wise people for their wisdom.

Elizabeth Gaskell

When you win, you're an old pro. When you lose, you're an old man.

Charley Conerly

As we grow older, we grow both more foolish and wiser at the same time.

La Rochefoucauld

In the depth of winter, I finally learned that within me there lay an invincible summer.

Albert Camus

H. L. Mencken told me once that he answered all his mail, pleasant and unpleasant, with just one line, 'You may be right.' That's the way I feel now. It is in the realm of possibility, just barely, that I could be the one who's wrong.

Clare Boothe Luce

You stay young as long as you can learn, acquire new habits and suffer contradiction.

Marie von Ebner-Eschenbach

The longer I live the more I see that I am never wrong about anything, and that all the pains that I have so humbly taken to verify my notions have only wasted my time.

George Bernard Shaw

The older you are the more slowly you read a contract.

Leonard Louis Levenson

I am an old man and have known a great many troubles, but most of them never happened.

Mark Twain

I suppose you think that persons who are as old as me are always thinking about very grave things, but I know that I am meditating on the same old themes that we did when we were 10 years old, only we go more gravely about it.

Henry David Thoreau

As I grow older, I have learned to read the papers calmly and not to hate the fools I read about.

Edmund Wilson

As I grow older, I pay less attention to what men say. I just watch what they do.

Andrew Carnegie

It's worth asking: What do you want? It gets harder and harder to answer as you get older. The answer gets subtler and subtler.

John Jerome

I have a simple philosophy: Fill what's empty. Empty what's full. And scratch where it itches.

Alice Roosevelt

One thing I've learned as I get older is to just go ahead and do it. It's much easier to apologize after something's been done than to get permission ahead of time.

Grace Murray Hopper

I seem to have been only like a boy playing on the seashore, and diverting myself in now and then finding a smoother pebble or a prettier shell than ordinary, whilst the great ocean of truth lay all undiscovered before me.

Isaac Newton

If by the time we are 60 we haven't learned what a knot of paradox and contradiction life is, and how exquisitely the good and bad are mingled in every action we take, we haven't grown old to much purpose.

John Cowper Powys

What a wonderful life I've had! How I wish I had realized it sooner.

Colette

Mottoes to Live By

If you wake up in the morning then you're ahead for the day.

Mace Neufield

You can't turn back the clock. But you can wind it up again.

Bonnie Prudden

Mottoes to Live By

You're never too old to become younger.

Mae West

It's never too late to be what you might have been.

George Eliot

I think, therefore I still am.

Elliott Priest

If you rest, you rust.

Helen Hayes

You're only old once!

Dr Seuss

Live well, learn plenty, laugh often, love much.

Ralph Waldo Emerson

If not now, when?

Hillel the Elder

Live your life as though your hair was on fire!

Anon

Learning and sex until rigor mortis!

Maggie Kuhn

Mottoes to Live By

To stop the ageing – keep on raging.

Malcolm Forbes

Never pass a bathroom.

Duke of Edinburgh

Don't take life so seriously. It's not permanent.

Kathy Holder

Exercise daily. Eat wisely. Die anyway.

Anon

May you live all the days of your life.

Jonathan Swift

Live your life and forget your age.

Norman Vincent Peale

May you live to be 100 and may the last voice you hear be mine.

Frank Sinatra

If you can't make it better, you can laugh at it.

Erma Bombeck

He who laughs, lasts.

Mary Pettibone Poole

Index

Index

Index

Index

Index

Index

Index

Index

Index

Index